PEDAGOGY OF COMPUTER LITERACY

PEDAGOGY OF COMPUTER LITERACY

An Indian Experience

BINOD C. AGRAWAL

Assisted by
Madhavi Joshi

CONCEPT PUBLISHING COMPANY, NEW DELHI - 110059

ISBN 81-7022-574-4

First Published 1996

Published and Printed by
Ashok Kumar Mittal
CONCEPT PUBLISHING COMPANY
A/15-16, Commercial Block, Mohan Garden,
NEW DELHI - 110059 (India)
Phones : 5554042, 5504042

PREFACE

This book emerged out of an evaluation commissioned by Department of Electronics, Government of India, 1984-85. We came in the picture because, the then Secretary, Department of Electronics, Mr. S.R. Vijaykar was keen to have an evaluation of the Computer Literacy and Studies in Schools (CLASS) project by an independent agency. Mr. Vijaykar was connected with the production of electronics for Satellite Instructional Television Experiment (SITE) in mid-seventies. He knew of our existence and some of us for several years. Hence, he sought help in this matter from Professor E.V. Chitnis, the then Director, Space Applications Centre, Ahmedabad. Initially, these two gentlemen discussed the possibility of the CLASS project social evaluation. It was followed by a series of meetings in which my colleagues, Mr. K.S. Karnik and Mr. B.S. Bhatia participated. On a crash basis, we developed an outline for an evaluation plan which was presented to Department of Electronics and the National Council for Educational Research and Training (NCERT) officials. As a parallel activity, we started exploring the possibility of joining hands with the Universities in several parts of the country to work on the total evaluation.

There were two major summative evaluations to be undertaken for CLASS project. For each, we had set up advisory committees. These committees met to operationalise evaluation aspects of the project. In view of the interdisciplinary nature of the project, a Core Group was set up to overview the CLASS evaluation. The Core Group consisted of computer experts, an economist, management experts and social scientists. The Core Group decided that each component of the CLASS evaluation would be undertaken by an expert within the Core Group. Professor U.K. Srivastava of the Indian Institute of Management, Ahmedabad was accordingly requested to help us in the cost benefit analysis of the project. Mr. Arup Dasgupta and Mr. B.S. Bhatia were requested to help analyse the hardware and management aspects of the study respectively. The qualitative and quantitative evaluative studies became my responsibility. In consultation with eminent anthropologists of the country, we were able to design the holistic evaluation which were eventually conducted by the individual anthropologists in their respective regions. Keeping in view the regional diversity and school management, six holistic evaluations were conducted. The surveys were conducted by our research team members.

The total effort of CLASS project evaluation required a great deal of cooperation, coordination and assistance in the field for data collection. In the data collection phase, apart from all the members of Core Group, Professor M.C. Sekhar of Indian Institute of Mass Communication, New Delhi helped us collect data from Srinagar. The analysis and report writing remained our responsibility.

The book is based on the following studies which were completed as a part of the Computer Literacy and Studies in Schools (CLASS) Evaluation :

1. Computer Demystification in School : An Evaluative Study by Binod C. Agrawal and Arbind K. Sinha, assisted by Radhika Mallick (June 1986).
2. Computer Impact on Students : An Evaluation by Binod C. Agrawal, Anita Kamdar and Sulbha Khanna (June 1986).
3. Computer Literacy and Studies in Schools (CLASS) Evaluation : An Interim Report (Anonymous, 1985).
4. Final Report on the Holistic Study of the CLASS Project at Allahabad by Shashank Misra (Project Director Gopala Sarana) 1987.
5. Computer Literacy and Studies in Schools (CLASS) in Delhi : An Evaluation of CLASS Project Through Holistic Study by Dr. J.S. Bhandari (June 1986).
6. Computer Literacy and Studies in Schools in Madras City: An Evaluation of the Pilot Phase of CLASS Project by N. Subba Reddy and G. Sujatha (1986).
7. Evaluation Report on the CLASS Project in Orissa by L.K. Mahapatra and Bandita Swain (1986).
8. Computer Literacy and Studies in Schools (CLASS) in Guwahati by Annada C. Bhagabati and Meenakshi Das (1986).
9. Computer Education in School (Evaluation of Computer Literacy and Studies in School Pilot Project: A Holistic Study) by R.B. Lal and Madhavi Joshi (1986).

All these studies were sponsored by Development and Educational Communication Unit, ISRO, Ahmedabad. They were financed by Department of Electronics, Government of India.

First and foremost, I am grateful to Mr. S.R. Vijaykar and Professor E.V. Chitnis for giving me this opportunity. Mr. K.S. Karnik provided all the administrative and academic support required to complete the work. I am thankful for his support. I am thankful to Professor A.K. Jalaluddin, NCERT, Mr. T.R. Raman, Joint Secretary, Department of Electronics and his team members, Mr. W.R. Deshpande and Mr. S.N. Jindal, both Joint Directors, who helped in this study. Mr. Vikram V. Desai, Consultant, Department of Electronics, did his best to ensure that our work was completed in time. My sincere thanks to him too. In the Department of Education, Ministry of Human Resource Development, two individuals, who not only took keen interest in this evaluation but also contributed in facilitating the work, were Mr. Y.N. Chaturvedi, Joint Secretary and Mr. R.S. Sirohi, Deputy Secretary, along with other staff. My sincere thanks to them.

The academic support of evaluation came from a number of friends and colleagues across the country. I would particularly like to mention Professors A.C. Bhagabati, J.S. Bhandari, Gopala Sarana, R.B. Lal, L.K. Mahapatra and N. Subba Reddy. They were assisted by Meenakshi Das, Madhavi Joshi, G. Sujatha, Shashank Misra, Sudhansu Misra and Bandita Swain. I am thankful to all of them for doing an excellent job and completing the individual reports in time for the preparation of consolidated report. For conducting the survey, Professors Snehlata Shukla, Vimal P. Shah, M.C. Sekhar, A.C. Sinha and P.M. Shinghi provided initial advice and helped designing the study. I am thankful to all of them for their assistance.

Dr. Rekha Jain of the Indian Institute of Management, Ahmedabad helped us in defining the meaning of "demystification" for this project. I am thankful for her most valuable assistance. In Ahmedabad, my colleagues, Mr. N. Sampath, Mr. B.S. Bhatia and Mr. S.R. Joshi helped in more than one way to conduct this study. I am thankful to all of them. My colleagues who shouldered the responsibility of this evaluation are Dr. Arbind K. Sinha, Dr. Sulbha Khanna, Anita Kamdar and Radhika Mullick. I am thankful to all of them for their untiring help to meet the deadlines. Omana Raghavan typed the reports. I am thankful to her.

One person who assisted throughout the preparation of this work is Madhavi Joshi. I am thankful to her for here painstaking effort to consolidate the holistic studies and other material. The final word processing was done by Neeta Kumar. Thanks are also due to Champa Gajera who initially provided assistance in word processing.

JANUARY 26, 1996 BINOD C. AGRAWAL

CLASS EVALUATION CORE GROUP

Binod C. Agrawal

B.S. Bhatia

A.R. Dasgupta*

S.R. Joshi

Anita Kamdar

K.S. Karnik

Sulbha Khanna

N. Sampath

Arbind Sinha

U.K. Srivastava

PROJECT RESEARCH TEAM

Binod C. Agrawal

Anita Kamdar

Sulbha Khanna

Radhika Mullick

Arbind Sinha

HOLISTIC STUDY TEAM

Binod C. Agrawal

Development and Educational Communication Unit Ahmedabad

Experts

A.C. Bhagabati
Guwahati University,
Guwahati.

J.S. Bhandari
University of Delhi,
New Delhi.

R.B. Lal
Gujarat Vidyapith,
Ahmedabad.

L.K. Mahapatra
Utkal University,
Bhubaneshwar.

N. Subba Reddy
University of Madras,
Madras.

Gopala Sarana
Lucknow University,
Lucknow.

Anthropologists

Meenakshi Das, Guwahati
Sudhansu Misra, Delhi
Madhavi Joshi, Ahmedabad
Bandita Swain, Bhubaneshwar
G. Sujatha, Madras
Shashank Misra, Allahabad

CONTENTS

LIST OF TABLES

INTRODUCTION

Computer is almost a household name in most of the Euro-American countries. Computers have carved an important niche for themselves with their wide ranging applications in various fields across the world. Computers have been introduced into the Asian countries quite recently, particularly in India. Since then, computers are being increasingly used in all aspects of social life in the country. Banks, Railways and the Airlines have already introduced computers in their day-to-day operational services. Besides, computers have also been introduced in large and small business organisations for maintenance of company records and accounts. The idea of introducing computers in schools in India is based on future needs wherein it is felt that computers are here to stay and will play an increasingly important role in social life. Hence, it is only appropriate that todays students to be so oriented as to adjust in a world largely dominated by computers.

Learning from the Past

The arguments for the introduction of computer literacy in India are many. However, the most powerful of them sees computers as essentials of life in an inevitably growing technological society. Skills on the computer have become as basic as those of reading and writing, so much so that the public ignorance of the subject constitutes a real crisis (Luehrmann 1987 : 98). Taking this argument as the basis, most research studies start with the unconscious assumption that computer literacy cannot be neglected in any educational system. A lot of research has gone into the study of Computer Assisted Instruction (CIA), which involves active role of computers in teaching. Tony Adams in his keynote address at CAL 1987 Symposium, uses

Taylor's model of tutor, tool and tutee as a framework to discuss the different ways in which computers can be used in the classroom. Most studies in the past have asked the question. "How effective is CAI ?" The "effectiveness" of CAI seems to be the pivot around which most studies on CAI revolve. The definition of "effectiveness" vary from the "amount of learning that takes place initially". . . to the "learners change in attitude toward the computer as an instructional medium or simply as a helpful tool in culture". (Chamber and Sprecher 1980 : 35 as quoted by Foreman 1980 : 37-50).

A study conducted by Ragosta, Holland and Jamison (1982 : 19-26) aimed to assess the effectiveness of three CAI curricula, mathematics, reading and language art. They observed that students, who worked on the mathematics curriculum, showed significantly better progress than those working on language art and reading. At another level, the study was designed to answer the much wider question of whether computers can be used as "Compensatory Educational Technique", fulfilling the demands of costs within a typical per student allocation. On the whole, the authors found their results favourable to CAI. Hartley (1977) using meta-analysis in a survey of mathematics CAI in elementary and secondary schools found that the gains for elementary students were more than gains for secondary students. Burns and Bozeman (1981 : 32-39) and Kulik (1981 : 32-39) got similar results on the validity of mathematics CAI.

It must be pointed out that most studies on CAI concentrated on testing the effectiveness of CAI on the subject of mathematics. Hence, it is difficult to make any general inferences about the viability and effectiveness of CAI in general. This is an important fact to consider while conducting any evaluation where every aspect of computer literacy must be studied in detail. It has also important bearings on the notion of "effectiveness" of CAI. For example, Fisher (1975 : 147-153) would argue that there are three significant factors for CAI effectiveness. These are "subject area", "student achievement range", and "setting".

Science and foreign language are the most effectively learnt subject areas with mathematics being moderately effective and reading and language art being least effective. The low and high achievers benefit the most through computers and CAI as a supplement to normal teaching is not effective. Instead, when integrated into the curriculum it could be very useful. Finally, the quality and appropriateness of CAI software is another major factor contributing to its effectiveness. Software that is not culture specific tends to hinder rather than facilitate the learning process.

As far as cost is concerned, Kearsley (1976 : 1-11) has pointed out that "economically the debate over the uses of CMI and CAI focuses on the (1) relative advantages that the computer has over traditional methods; (2) whether in fact less expensive means are available to effect the same instructional gains as the computer and (3) whether technological advances have reduced the costs to a point where school districts can implement computer based instruction." In case of India, these issues assume greater importance in view of the fact that all children in the school going age do not get chance to go to school.

The Current Debate

A new trend is being observed in research studies on the use of computers in education. Currently, scholars are arguing for a fresh input both in evaluation as well as in the use of computer based technologies. Kling (1984 : 127-147) attempted to synthesize the technological and the humanistic approaches to any assessment of computer based learning. He argues for a social impact analysis of computer literacy starting from the initial stages of computer software preparation, assessment and application in all fields. Giving examples from fields as diverse as social work, auditing and education, Kling points out that in many instances the introduction of Computer Based Packages (CBP) has not led to the utopian efficiency that advocates of the micro millennium had hoped for. It is for this reason that he argues against the normal cost benefit analysis based on a "MBA rationality" of cutting immediate costs and emphasizing technical feasibility. On the contrary, Kling thinks that the social dimensions are important.

Kling's emphasis on social factors is echoed in Jernstedt's (1985: 96-101) plea for "Computer Enhanced Collaborative Learning" (CECL). CECL is really a creative combination of CAI and cooperative interpersonal relations; an approach where the machine is not an anathema and active student-teacher, student-peer and student-student cooperation and interaction is encouraged. So, instead of a scenario where students sit isolated in front of a computer terminal, a group of students are attached to a computer terminal and learn through discussion. Recent research in education has thrown up the importance of an active interaction amongst students. Also, the cooperative mode of learning is deemed superior to either the competitive or the individualized one.

Computer Education in India

There seems to be differing motivations for the introduction of computers in school education at the higher secondary level or in the first twelve years of school education in India. It is well reflected in the report of the National Workshop on Computer Literacy Curriculum held at the National Council of Educational Research and Training (NCERT), New Delhi, on March 26-27, 1984. During the deliberations at the workshop, Chandra (1984 : vii) felt that "Anybody who grows up in the world of tomorrow, not knowing computers, not understanding computers, not being able to use them, will be lost, and that country which does not prepare its citizens to be fully familiar and conversant with computers, their technologies and their applications would not be able to keep its place in the industrial hierarchy in the community of nations". Others felt that "...introduction of computer literacy programme would have a liberalizing influence in schools, by making teachers sensitive to and ultimately capable of utilizing the computer for improving the effectiveness of instruction..." (1984 : 3). Malhotra (1984 : 9) thought that "computer literacy should either enable pupils to learn regular subjects better, or help him acquire some additional important skills having greater employment potential". The participants to the workshop thought that the aim of the computer literacy project should be to test "...the use of computers as an educational tool for improvement of quality of education" (Report of the National Workshop on Computer Literacy Curriculum held at NCERT on 26-27 March, 1984 : 11). However, the participants were clear that computer literacy was not meant for teaching students computer sciences or computer programming.

During the workshop, it was felt that:

"(a) Computer education should be introduced at senior secondary level and may gradually be introduced at middle and primary levels;

(b) Computer education would be a part of the curriculum for every student irrespective of the area he selects for specialisation; and

(c) Computer literacy programme would familiarize students with the computer as a versatile tool with immense application potential in all aspects of human development." (Report on the National Workshop on Computer Literacy Curriculum held at NCERT on 26-27 March, 1984 : 10).

The Computer Literacy and Studies in Schools (CLASS) project envisaged the use of computer as an educational tool and in the process improve the quality of education. However, CLASS was to be a voluntary non-examination subject which was open to students of all ability levels in secondary and higher secondary schools.

Computer Literacy and Studies in Schools (CLASS) Project

Considering the importance of computer education, the Department of Electronics, Government of India, in close cooperation with the Department of Education, Ministry of Human Resource Development, Government of India, launched a pilot project known as Computer Literacy and Studies in Schools (CLASS). National Council of Educational Research and Training (NCERT), New Delhi, took up the executive responsibility while the Indian Institute of Technology (IIT), New Delhi provided initial inputs for the implementation of CLASS project in terms of designing teachers' and students' training curriculum. CMC Limited had the responsibility to install and maintain the computers.

CLASS project was launched in July 1984 in a representative sample of 250 schools spread all over the country. The second phase was to cover 500 more schools. By 1989, there were about 2000 higher secondary schools having computers in the country. Although, the number of schools (250) included in the first phase was felt to be rather small considering the large number of secondary schools in the country (52,500 during 1981-82), it was agreed that at the initial stage it would be desirable to make a modest beginning. From that point of view, 250 schools could be regarded as a reasonable number where the experimental phase of the programme could be introduced in a variety of educational institutions.

While identifying schools for participation in the CLASS pilot project, the Department of Electronics and Department of Education were extremely careful. After close consultation with the State education authorities and other agencies concerned with school education, like the Kendriya Vidyalaya Sangathan (KVS), Central Board of Secondary Education (CBSE) and NCERT, the schools were drawn from Kendriya Vidyalayas, Government schools affiliated with CBSE, State Board schools and private schools. Both boys, girls and co-educational schools were selected. The programme was to consist of about 30 lectures of one hour duration and 30 practical sessions each two hours long.

The experiences gained from CLASS project were to provide a good amount of basic information for :

"(a) determining the feasibility of expanding the coverage of the programme in the Seventh and subsequent Five-Year Plans;

(b) identifying problems which will require to be attended to, particularly when the coverage of the programme would be expanded;

(c) identifying the changes that would be required in educational management structures with a view to incorporating the computer as an essential tool for education; and

(d) identifying the modifications that would require to be made in the implementation strategy" (Report of the National Workshop on Computer Literacy Curriculum held at NCERT on 26-27 March, 1984 : 4).

The main objectives of the CLASS project, as identified in the report of the National Workshop on Computer Literacy Curriculum, held in March 1984 was as follows :

"(a) provide students with a broad understanding of computers and their use;

(b) familiarize students with the range of computer applications in all walks of human activity and potentiality of the computer as an information processing tools;

(c) demystify computers and develop a degree of ease and familiarity with computers which would be conducive to developing individual creativity in identifying and developing applications relevant to the immediate environment of the child" (Report of the National Workshop on Computer Literacy Curriculum held at NCERT on 26-27 March, 1984 : 3).

CLASS Project Evaluation

CLASS being a pilot project, involved about 250 schools scattered all over the country, and under different types of administrative set ups, it was natural that the extent of information gain would differ depending on the type of school and the other facilities available. For the purpose of measuring computer knowledge gain among students and level of demystification, an independent evaluation of the project was thought essential.

The current research debate on computer discussed earlier is important from the point of view the CLASS project evaluation in the Indian context. The fallacy of a "technology centered" analysis of computer in education must be replaced by an indepth analysis of social and cultural factors involved in the use of computer aided instruction in schools. The review of literature showed that the notion of computer education is now an accepted one in the Euro-American countries. However, it must be pointed out that most of the studies on Computer Aided Instruction have originated in the Euro-American context. And the Euro-American scenario is distinctly different from the Indian one. It was, therefore, necessary that the evaluation of CLASS project must be board and should be able to provide answers to most of the questions raised earlier. So the approach to CLASS project evaluation was decided to be *inter* and *multi* disciplinary, involving computer experts, educationists, social scientists, electronics engineers, planning and management experts.

In order to formulate the operational aspects of the CLASS evaluation and evaluation objectives, two meeting were called during February and June, 1985. In these meetings representatives of Department of Electronics and NCERT, experts from the Indian Institute of Management, Ahmedabad, Gujarat University, Ahmedabad, and anthropologists from various universities participated. The evaluation proposals prepared by the evaluation team were discussed in detail. These experts after detailed discussion approved the evaluation proposals and evaluation objectives with few modifications. It was also agreed that holistic studies as well as survey will be conducted for the evaluation of the CLASS project. Evaluation objectives were accordingly defined for both kinds of studies.

Objectives of Evaluation

The holistic study focussed its attention on CLASS project evaluation keeping in view two broad and inter-related objectives, which aimed:

(a) to determine the extent to which the goal of demystification was met; and

(b) to analyze various aspects of the CLASS project so as to provide guidelines for the proposed expansion plan.

On the other hand, the survey was aimed to find out :

(a) the extent to which demystification took place as a result of the CLASS project introduction in the higher secondary schools/colleges;

(b) to assess the computer learning due to its exposure among the students;

(c) to investigate the level of familiarization with the range of computer applications among the students;

(d) to assess the influence of computer among the teachers and school system and their attitudes towards computer;

(e) to compare and contrast factors influencing the learning of computer in terms of sex, socio-economic background and class performance of the students at the individual level, and type of school, medium of instruction, stream and region at the contextual level; and

(f) to investigate the difficulties or problems arising as a result of foreign software on the learning process of students.

A careful comparison indicated that both these studies essentially were geared to measure the demystification of computer and its related aspects. The methods and techniques followed for CLASS evaluation using two separate methods will be discussed in the following chapters.

2

HOLISTIC APPROACH TO CLASS EVALUATION

CLASS project in its scope was multi-disciplinary involving high technology, different educational systems and implementing agencies. The evaluation of such a project required a wide ranging study necessitating a variety of approaches, experts and research methods and techniques. Two methods followed for CLASS evaluation included 'holistic' and survey methods. Each has been described separately. In this chapter holistic method will be discussed while in Chapter 3 survey method will be discussed.

Based on the experiences gained during the Satellite Instructional Television Experiment (SITE) social evaluation, it was felt that CLASS project must be studied and analyzed in its totality for a qualitative and indepth understanding of the process of computer education (Agrawal 1985). Further, the process of learning induced through an educational technology innovation (computer) must be investigated within the cultural milieu. Keeping this view in mind, an inter-disciplinary and multi-disciplinary approaches to CLASS evaluation was considered essential as indicated in Chapter 1. In the recent educational programme evaluations, an added emphasis has been laid on the qualitative and indepth evaluation, in addition to quantitative evaluation. Also, 'participant observation' used in anthropological researches has been considered as most desirable to discern truth and validate the information collected through verbal responses. CLASS being a pilot project, an exploratory study was designed for this purpose. There were several steps to be followed for conducting CLASS holistic evaluation, those being :

(a) to decide the number of such studies to be conducted to

be considered representative of the 250 schools spread all over the country, and selection of locales for the field data collection;

(b) methods and techniques to be followed in data collection;

(c) nature and quality of data to be collected;

(d) defined areas in which focus be directed towards obtaining answers to the specific questions of the evaluation; and

(e) the comparative method to be utilized for preparing an integrated report from a number of holistic studies conducted at various locations in different educational settings.

The broad objectives indicated in Chapter 1 were further amplified and detailed out by the anthropologists who participated in the February 1985 workshop, specially convened for this purpose. As these anthropologists belonged to different regions of the country, they helped in providing a very broad canvas for CLASS project evaluation and in the finalizing the outline of the holistic evaluation.

Selection of Evaluative Study Locations

Keeping in view the socio-cultural and educational diversity at the higher secondary level, it was felt that any study that could provide a national perspective must have a fair representation of the diversity. The first and foremost factor considered was that there should be a fair representation of 'school types' in terms of management. In other words, the study locale should have schools belonging to Kendriya Vidyalaya Sangathan, State Educational Board (both state and privately managed) having medium of instruction in state language and Hindi/ English. Second, the locations should have representation of metropolitan, medium and small size cities. Third, the anthropologists interested in this kind of evaluative study should be available and willing to collaborate.

After consultation with several anthropologists, who participated in the February 1985 meeting, six cities were selected with each having more than four CLASS schools belonging to different educational systems. The cities were distributed in three population categories. Delhi (Union Territory) and Madras (Tamil Nadu) represented two metropolitan cities of north and south regions, whereas Ahmedabad (Gujarat) and Guwahati (Assam) belonged to medium sized cities of west and north-east regions. Allahabad (Uttar Pradesh) and Bhubaneshwar (Orissa) belonged to third category of small sized cities in the northern and eastern regions respectively. Table 2.1 shows the distribution of CLASS project schools both within the state and in each city. It is apparent from Table 2.1 that little over 20 per cent CLASS project schools have been covered by these six cities for holistic evaluation. For the convenience of description and analysis, each city for the CLASS project holistic evaluation will be referred to as "study cluster". Within each "study cluster", as indicated in Table 2.1, there are on an average 8.5 schools under CLASS project in which the number of schools in Delhi comes to 20, that being 40 per cent of the total 51 schools.

A methodological question raised was whether all the schools in each city should be covered or the number be limited for detailed participant observation. Keeping in view the human limitation, it was decided that at least two schools in each study cluster belonging to two different educational systems will be selected for this purpose. At the same time, it was thought appropriate to have detailed information about all the schools falling under each study cluster.

TABLE 2.1 : Distribution of CLASS Schools in Holistic Evaluation Study Clusters

Sr. No.	Name of the City	State	No. of CLASS Schools in the State	No. of CLASS Schools in the City
1.	Ahmedabad	Gujarat	15	7
2.	Allahabad	U.P.	27	5
3.	Bhubaneshwar	Orissa	10	5
4.	Delhi	Delhi	20	20
5.	Guwahati	Assam	10	5
6.	Madras	Tamil Nadu	16	9
	Total		98	51

Table 2.2 provides the list of the selected CLASS schools for holistic evaluation. Table 2.2 shows that out of 12 schools, four belong to Kendriya Vidyalays Sangathan whereas the remaining belong to their respective State Education Boards, managed by State or various private organizations. It may be mentioned that in Madras, one of the selected schools had to be substituted by another. The reason was that in this particular school computer classes were held to teach students who had offered computer science as an elective/optional course and not under CLASS project.

TABLE 2.2 : List of Selected Schools By Management and Type*

Name of the Study cluster	Management	School Type
Ahmedabad		
1. Kendriya Vidyalaya No. 1, Shahibaug	KVS**	Co-educational
2. Diwan Ballubhai Madhyamik Shala, Maninagar	Private Trust	Co-educational
Allahabad		
3. Kendriya Vidyalaya, Manauri	KVS	Co-educational
4. D.P. Girls Inter College, Katra	State Aided	Girls
Bhubaneshwar		
5. Kendriya Vidyalaya No. 1	KVS	Co-educational
6. Demonstration Multi-purpose School	NCERT	Co-educational
Delhi		
7. Andhra Education Society Senior Secondary School, Rouse Avenue	State Aided	Co-educational
8. Government Girls' Senior Secondary School No. 2, Roop Nagar	Government	Girls
Guwahati		
9. T.C. Government Girls' Higher Secondary and Multi-purpose School	Government	Girls
10. Kendriya Vidyalaya, Khanapara	KVS	Co-educational
Madras		
11. Kendriya Vidyalaya, CLRI	KVS	Co-educational
12. Corporation Higher Secondary School for Girls, Nungambakkam	State Board of Education	Girls

* In some states, like in Uttar Pradesh, a higher secondary school is referred to as Intermediate College.

** Kendriya Vidyalaya Sangathan.

Methods and Techniques of Data Collection

The holistic evaluation was designed to provide indepth qualitative understanding of the process of computer introduction in various educational systems, its effects and future implications. Hence, the method of the holistic study required not merely a comprehensive coverage of different and often seemingly unrelated aspects of computer literacy but also an indepth probing into these aspects to understand the "whole". Therefore, it necessitated consideration and investigation of a variety of internal and external factors and situations beyond CLASS project.

The field work in all the six study clusters began between the months of August and November, 1985 or the academic year, 1985-86 and was terminated in May 1986. The method of data collection followed by all anthropologists was generally uniform. The first few weeks were utilized in establishing rapport and familiarization with the setting of each school. For this purpose, frequent visits to the schools were undertaken. The anthropologists based at Delhi and Bhubaneshwar used questionnaires to collect the initial information, while at the other four places, techniques of informal interviewing and observation were applied.

The initial visits also helped in selecting the two schools for intensive study. The parameters used for the selection of schools for intensive study were the type of management, socio-economic background of pupils, attitude of the school principal, attitudes and reactions of the teachers, aptitude of students, basis of selection for students, number of students and the degree of interest of students in CLASS project. The anthropologists at Guwahati and Ahmedabad attended the CLASS Basic Training Course meant for computer teachers at their respective Resource Centres. Participation in the training programme not only gave them the required operational expertise of a computer teacher, but also provided them with an opportunity for "participant observation" of the responses and reactions of the computer teachers to the training programme and CLASS project. These anthropologists also studied side by side, the functioning of the Resource Centre.

Before going into details of the work-schedule followed by the anthropologists, it would be necessary to know how rapport with various agencies and schools was established. "The anthropological convention of working one's way from top downwards in a field situation was followed in the first contact visits to ...schools" (Bhagabati and Das 1986:33). The heads of institutions were contacted first by the anthropologists followed by the teachers and students. As the anthropologists were connected with universities, it was not difficult for them to prove their credentials.

The work schedule followed by the anthropologists was worked out in accordance with the school time table. Schools were visited during the computer class timings for the purpose of participant observation during computer classes. The remaining time was utilized in studying the school environment and its various components like the management, principal, teachers and students. The inter-relationships and interactions between the various agencies involved in the CLASS project, such as the CMC, Resource Centre, State Education Department officials were also studied. "Anthropological techniques of research such as observation, structured and unstructured interviews, informal conversations, recording of case-studies were all employed in the course of this evaluative study" (Subba Reddy and Sujatha 1986:9). Certain quantitative data were collected through questionnaires or interview schedules. In addition, various types of documents such as correspondence and records available with the schools were referred. Informal visits to homes of students were undertaken to collect information regarding familial background of students for which unstructured but guided interview technique was used in all the study clusters except Bhubaneshwar where a structured interview schedule was used to interview parents of computer students. Home visits were usually conducted on holidays or during afternoon.

Data on the functioning of computer, its utilisation by the students and repair and maintenance records were also collected. The anthropologists maintained a regular work diary throughout the period of study.

Nature and Quality of Data

As indicated earlier in each study cluster, two schools were intensively studied, thereby covering 12 schools for providing detailed data on CLASS project. Intensive interaction in these schools yielded indepth information and insights into the actual operation and working of the CLASS project. Further, quantitative data were collected to supplement the qualitative observations. In this respect, it was possible to collect reliable and high quality data verified by repeated checking and rechecking. While efforts were made by anthropologists to collect as much data as possible about CLASS project, it was thought most desirable to have few aspects of the project studied in greater detail. These included selected case studies of students, their parents and teachers. Some efforts were also made to study the different educational systems followed in the States of Assam, Gujarat, Orissa, Tamil Nadu and Utter Pradesh. Educational systems of Directorate of Education, Delhi and Kendriya Vidyalaya Sangathan were also studied.

Problems During Fieldwork

Operating in the field was not all smooth sailing for the anthropologists. Each study cluster had its share of problems. One of the common difficulties concerned access to the computer teachers, principals and in some cases the computer room. A lot of time was usually spent in just getting in touch with these individuals. An unwillingness on the part of most of the principals, to accommodate the enquiries of the anthropologists was observed. It was felt that they were either busy or appeared a little hesitant to talk because of the indifferent way in which CLASS project was running in some schools. The anthropologists in some places were also initially considered as a "management person" who could not be trusted. Thus, there was a tendency to get rid of the anthropologists as early as possible. Difficulty in access to computer class was faced only by the anthropologists at Allahabad in case of a girls' school where the teachers seemed to object to the idea of his visiting the computer class. Another common problem faced was the time period which limited the scope of the study to a great extent. Also, the schools being placed at far-off distances, commuting to and fro consumed a lot of time.

Each study cluster also had certain specific problem areas. The field study in Guwahati suffered a great deal as a result of cancellation of classes due to electricity failure. The study at Madras faced a number of interruptions due to school agitations and heavy rains causing floods. The field study in Ahmedabad took off late due to delayed reopening of schools following riots in the city.

CLASS project being an experiment, the presence of anthropologists in the six study clusters affected the natural experimental situation. The very presence of the anthropologists in the selected schools disturbed the climate in several ways. Important among these were increased activity for CLASS project, higher participation of the computer teachers, greater awareness about the project among the principals, teachers and the students. Almost everywhere anthropologists reported that some of the computer related activities were performed because of their presence. In Madras, for example, the anthropologist reported that at one of the schools the two computer teachers were totally ignorant of the number of software packages provided to the school or even the presence of the NCERT booklet and other user-guide manuals. In Guwahati and Bhubaneshwar, it was reported that due to several visits of the anthropologists, the computer room was made operational.

In this chapter, the actual method and techniques followed for the holistic evaluation have been discussed. In the following chapter, survey approach of the class evaluation will be presented.

3

SURVEY APPROACH TO CLASS EVALUATION

In order to have quantitative understanding of CLASS project for generalization and planning, it was considered essential to conduct several surveys to investigate the functioning of CLASS project using descriptive survey design. As a part of process evaluation, two such surveys were conducted during the academic year 1985-86. In addition, as a part of summative evaluation, it was decided to conduct a survey using field experimental design. Both experimental (computer) and control (non-computer) students, were to be selected for "before" and "after" data collection to measure the degree of demystification and students' level of broad understanding of computers. However, the same could not be done because all CLASS schools did not start functioning in the beginning of academic year 1985-86. So a cross-sectional research design was suggested. In the alternative design, only one set of data were to be collected at the end of the academic year 1985-86. Four major areas of investigations proposed included students, teachers, principals (representing the schools management) and Resource Centres. The broad objectives of survey are indicated in Chapter 1.

Descriptive Survey Design

A descriptive survey design was used for data collection in order to cover the entire 250 schools.* This was considered necessary as it happened to be a unique experiment and the aim was to know the

* In all, 250 schools were to be covered in the survey. But the list provided by Department of Electronics had only 249 schools. Hence 249 schools were approached for data collection.

installation status of the computer. As the schools were dispersed all over the country, it became extremely difficult to collect first hand data through personal interviews. Therefore, a "mail questionnaire" was utilized for data collection. This questionnaire was sent to 231 principals of CLASS schools whose complete postal addresses were available with us in March 1985. Out of 231 schools, during a span of ten weeks (March-May, 1985), 164 principals returned the completed questionnaire. Participation in CLASS related seminars and workshops arranged by NCERT, New Delhi, provided insights into the functioning of the CLASS project. Also, some efforts were made to have detailed discussion with key officials of the Department of Electronics and Department of Education, Government of India, directly involved in the CLASS project including the Secretary of the Department of Electronics.

A similar survey was repeated to provide feedback on the functioning and utilization of various components of the CLASS project at the school level. For this purpose 182 principals out of 250 schools and 580 teachers of these schools were contacted through mail questionnaire in September-October 1985. Replies of 89 principals and 185 teachers representing 106 schools were received.

Cross-Sectional Design

A cross-sectional design was utilized for the third and final round of survey. This time while majority of the computer teachers, principals and Resources Centres were approached through mail questionnaire, a selected number of teachers, principals Resource Centres and selected CLASS or computer students and non-CLASS or non-computer students were contacted in person for data collection. In the following section an attempt will be made to discuss details of the third survey.

Sampling of Cross-Sectional Survey

Keeping the magnitude of problems and diversity, number of schools and students, type of schools, geographical distribution and medium of instruction, a multi-level stratified random sample was drawn for the selection of 24 out of 250 schools for the final survey. Accordingly, six regions comprising of twelve cities (two from each region) were selected. Among the selected cities, six cities were same as those for the holistic evaluation study (Table 2.1). In this way at the first level of sampling, the 12 cities selected represented 11 States and a Union Territory to form 12 "survey clusters". In each survey cluster on an average there were more than four CLASS project schools (Table 3.1).

TABLE 3.1 : Distribution of CLASS Schools in Survey Cluster

Sr. No.	Name of the City	State	No. of CLASS Schools in the State	No. of CLASS Schools in the City
1.	Ahmedabad*	Gujarat	15	14
2.	Allahabad	U.P.	27	5
3.	Bhopal	M.P.	15	8
4.	Bhubaneshwar	Orissa	10	4
5.	Delhi	Delhi	20	20
6.	Guwahati	Assam	10	5
7.	Jaipur	Rajasthan	9	4
8.	Madras	Tamil Nadu	16	9
9.	Mysore	Karnataka	10	4
10.	Ranchi	Bihar	11	4
11.	Srinagar/Jammu	Jammu & Kashmir	5	3
12.	Warangal	Andhra Pradesh	11	3
	Total		159	83

* Baroda and Gandhinagar are included

At the second level of sampling, from each of the "survey cluster" two schools were selected from among the CLASS project schools located in that survey cluster. Care was taken to have an appropriate representation, from different kind of medium of instruction and management type in the sample. Originally 22 schools were selected for conducting the survey, in which eight belonged to Kendriya Vidyalaya Sangathan, seven were State Government run schools, and remaining seven included schools run by Public or Private Charitable Trust and Zilla Parishad or Corporation. Later, Srinagar was included in the survey cluster to represent the Northern most region. In this way, 24 schools were selected for conducting the survey.

During data collection, one school each from three cities namely Madras, Jaipur and Mysore, were dropped from the sample due to non-availability of students. In order to compensate, one school from Gandhinagar and one from Baroda were added to the sample. Thus the final sample had 23 schools out of which 12 were Kendriya Vidyalayas/Demonstration Multipurpose Schools, six were state government schools, and five were Public/Private and Zilla Parishad/ Corporation Schools.

In each of the 12 survey clusters, one controlled school was selected after matching this school with one of the two schools of the CLASS school in terms of management type, medium of instruction and educational stream namely, science, arts and commerce (Tables 3.2 and 3.3).

TABLE 3.2 : Distribution of Control Schools in Survey Cluster According to Management and Medium of Instruction

Sr. No.	Name of City	Management and Medium of Instruction in School				
		Kendriya Vidyalaya/ NCERT	State Govern-ment	Private/Public Govt. aided		Total
		English+ Hindi	Hindi/ State language	Hindi/ State lang.**	English+ Hindi/ State lang.**	
1.	Ahmedabad*	2	1	1	–	4
2.	Allahabad	1	–	1	–	2
3.	Bhopal	1	1	–	–	2
4.	Bhubaneshwar	2	–	–	–	2
5.	Delhi	1	1	–	–	2
6.	Guwahati	1	1	–	–	2
7.	Jaipur	1	–	–	–	1
8.	Madras	–	1	–	–	1
9.	Mysore	1	–	–	–	1
10.	Ranchi	–	2	–	–	2
11.	Srinagar/Jammu	2	–	–	–	2
12.	Warangal	–	1	–	1	2
	Total	12	8	2	1	23

* Baroda and Gandhinagar are included.
** Language.

At the third level of sampling, individual students were to be selected for interview. Keeping in view the number of students in CLASS project, in each of the 24 CLASS project schools, 30 students were selected from among the computer students. An equal number of students were selected from the same school as non-computer students. Same sampling procedure was followed for selecting 30 students in each of the 12 control schools. Sample was randomly drawn while selecting the students. It is important to point out that in several CLASS project schools there were less than 30 students enrolled in the CLASS project. Hence, the entire class was selected for data collection. Table 3.4 provides the sample distribution of computer students.

TABLE 3.3 : Distribution of Control Schools in Survey Cluster According to Management and Medium of Instruction

Sr. No.	Name of City	Management and Medium of Instruction					Total
		Kendriya Vidyalaya/	State Government	Private & Government Aided			
		English+ Hindi	Hindi/ State lang.	English	Hindi/ State lang.**	English+ Hindi/ State lang.	
1.	Ahmedabad*	–	–	1	1	–	2
2.	Allahabad	1	–	–	–	–	1
3.	Bhopal	–	1	–	–	–	1
4.	Bhubaneshwar	–	–	–	–	1	1
5.	Delhi	–	1	–	–	–	1
6.	Guwahati	–	–	–	–	–	0
7.	Jaipur	–	–	1	–	–	1
8.	Madras	–	1	–	–	–	1
9.	Mysore	–	–	–	1	–	1
10.	Ranchi	–	–	–	1	–	1
11.	Srinagar/Jammu	1	–	–	–	–	1
12.	Warangal	–	–	–	1	–	1
	Total	2	3	2	4	1	12

* Baroda and Gandhinagar are included.

** Language.

TABLE 3.4 : Distribution of Computer Students in Survey Cluster

Sr. No.	Name of City	Original Sample		Final Sample	
		No. of Schools	No. of Students	No. of Schools	No. of Students
1.	Ahmedabad*	2	60	4*	95
2.	Allahabad	2	60	2	38
3.	Bhopal	2	60	2	59
4.	Bhubaneshwar	2	60	2	47
5.	Delhi	2	60	2	52
6.	Guwahati	2	60	1	30
7.	Jaipur	2	60	1	30
8.	Madras	2	60	1	30
9.	Mysore	2	60	1	21
10.	Ranchi	2	60	2	58
11.	Srinagar/Jammu	2	60	2	42
12.	Warangal	2	60	2	42
	Total	24	720	22	544

* Baroda and Gandhinagar are included.

Instrument Development

All instruments for the survey were constructed in English language because the medium of instruction for CLASS was English. It was expected that each student would have at least a working knowledge of English language in order to participate in CLASS project. Same holds true for the teachers, principals and Resource Centres. For process evaluation two sets of questionnaires were developed in English for each phase of the study. Questionnaires were designed for principals, computer teachers and Resource Centres. During Summative evaluation six questionnaires were designed for six separate sets of respondents. These were: (a) computer student; (b) non-computer student in computer school; (c) control student; (d) computer teacher; (e) principal; and (f) Resource Centre. Each of these questionnaires was pretested in four survey clusters. Based on the pretesting, the final instruments were developed.

Procedure of Data Collection

In the process evaluation phase of data collection introduction letter along with pre-paid self addressed envelopes were sent with all mail questionnaires. Data collection of the summative evaluation survey was a team effort in which members of research team visited various schools for this purpose. A brief introduction explaining the purpose of the survey was given. Afterwards, students were assembled in a classroom where questionnaires were distributed and filled in the group. It was observed that students of non-English medium schools had difficulty in filling the questionnaire. In such a situation, the researcher or a person conversant with the local language, generally a member of the team helped in translating questions for the students. This was a uniform problem in all the 24 schools. A similar procedure was followed for data collection from non-computer students and control school students. In spite of this difficulty the students were fairly enthusiastic in filling the questionnaires though, March-April 1986 being the fag end of the academic year, many students had stopped coming to schools in order to prepare for final examination. This was also one of the reasons that no data could be collected from three schools of Jaipur, Mysore and Madras.

In order to have first-hand information from the principals, computer teachers and coordinators of Resource Centres in all the 12 survey clusters, questionnairs were handed over to them personally. Generally, it was observed that there was a reluctance to provide detailed information about computer use as there was low utilization of computers. In case of principals, it seems, majority of them genuinely had very little first hand information about the working of the project. Hence, they asked the research team members to wait before filling the questionnaire. In case of Resource Centre coordinators, the difficult part was to meet them. The final sample included 26 out of 42 Resource Centre coordinators, 125 principals out of 250. Table 3.5 provides a sample distribution of non-computer students. Table 3.6 provides a distribution of control students.

As indicated in Table 3.4, 544 questionnaires out of 720 as originally desired were filled. Out of 720 computer teachers, who were contacted for this study, only 335 questionnaires were received. Out of 335 questionnaires received, 11 questionnaires were rejected as the same were filled twice by the computer teachers.

TABLE 3.5 : Distribution of Non-computer Students in Survey Cluster

Sr. No.	Name of City	Original Sample		Final Sample	
		No. of Schools	No. of Students	No. of Schools	No. of Students
1.	Ahmedabad*	2	60	4	89
2.	Allahabad	2	60	2	34
3.	Bhopal	2	60	2	48
4.	Bhubaneshwar	2	60	2	31
5.	Delhi	2	60	2	54
6.	Guwahati	2	60	1	12
7.	Jaipur	2	60	1	30
8.	Madras	2	60	1	30
9.	Mysore	2	60	0	00
10.	Ranchi	2	60	2	64
11.	Srinagar/Jammu	2	60	2	49
12.	Warangal	2	60	2	69
	Total	24	720	21	510

* Baroda and Gandhinagar are included.

As the comparison between computer students and non-computer students drawn from CLASS project schools showed contrasting pictures of demystification, it was thought futile to compare the data with control students. Hence, only the data from experimental (computer) and control (non-computer) students were analyzed and presented in Chapter 7.

TABLE 3.6 : Distribution of Control Students in Survey Cluster

Sr. No.	Name of City	Original Sample	Final Sample
1.	Ahmedabad*	30	63
2.	Allahabad	30	12
3.	Bhopal	30	33
4.	Bhubaneshwar	30	30
5.	Delhi	30	35
6.	Guwahati	30	00
7.	Jaipur	30	34
8.	Madras	30	30
9.	Mysore	30	15
10.	Ranchi	30	33
11.	Srinagar/Jammu	30	30
12.	Warangal	30	32
	Total	360	347

* Baroda and Gandhinagar are included.

Analysis

The entire data were computerized for analysis. Data from all the three surveys have also been utilized in the preparation of the final book. For the purpose of presentation, three categories of schools by management type have been used. These are: (a) Kendriya Vidyalaya which includes three NCERT run Demonstration Multi-purpose Schools; (b) the State schools including all the government schools of that state and other schools run by the Zilla Parishad and the Corporation; and (c) the Private/Public or Government aided schools.

Operational Definitions

In order to have comparable data from the field, it is considered necessary to operationally define some of the key concepts used in this evaluation.

Demystification

One of the most important objectives of CLASS project was to "demystify" the students about computers. After serious discussions with several experts and persons involved in the project, the concept of demystification was operationalised after our first workshop and in consultation with Dr. Rekha Jain, from the Indian Institute of Management, Ahmedabad. Accordingly, a student will be considered demystified, if

1. the student is able to identify the computer; if he/she is conversant with the operation mechanism of the keyboard, floppy, monitor, central processing unit, storage, screens, memory and the input-output of a computer;
2. the student is able to execute a software programme which is stored in the memory and goes to the processing unit for execution;
3. the student is acquainted with the limitations of the computer; and
4. the student is aware of the varied applications of the computer.

Unit of Analysis

Each school under study has been treated as an unit of analysis in this book. Hence, comparisons have been among the schools of various regions.

School/College

To minimize any semantic problem, throughout this book the term school will indicate Higher Secondary School, Intermediate College as used in different states of India for 10 + 2 system of education.

Computer Teachers

The teachers selected for computer training and teaching by the school management have been referred to as computer teachers in this study.

Computer Students

The students selected for CLASS project have been referred to as computer students.

4

PROFILE OF COMPUTER SCHOOLS

So far our discussions centred around the two methods followed for the evaluation of CLASS project. The cultural context for the introduction of computer was Higher Secondary School. Hence, it is necessary to have some understanding of the schools in India where these computers were installed. Based on the case studies, profile of the selected schools is presented in this chapter. Twelve schools selected for this purpose belong to six states of the country and represent defferent educational systems existing in these states.

Ahmedabad (Gujarat)

1. *Kendriya Vidyalaya No. 1, Shahibaug*

Kendriya Vidyalaya No. 1, established in 1964, is one of the three Kendriya Vidyalayas in Ahmedabad. The school does not have its own building and is presently housed in an old State Government owned building. The campus is spread out in a large area having four buildings. The offices of the principal and the vice-principal and administration are in one building also having the residential quarters of the principal. The classrooms and library function in a double storeyed building. The third building comprises of three science laboratories and the fourth building has the Socially Useful and Productive Work (SUPW) room and the computer room. A large playground surrounds the school buildings.

The school, which has English as medium of instruction, offers three streams at the Higher Secondary level, namely, Science, Humanities and Commerce. There are at present 1200 students enrolled in the school. Apart from the Principal, there are 66 teachers, most of whom are highly qualified and trained. The students generally belong to families with a good educational and economic background. Most of them belong to families of Central Government employees, Central Government undertakings and Armed Forces. They are a cosmopolitan group with very few Gujarati speaking students.

The school has over the years achieved a reputation of being a good school. There is a great deal of emphasis on a better than average result of students in public examinations. As a result, any innovation that may in some way affect the performance of the students in their examinations and thus threaten the reputation of the school is not encouraged.

2. *Diwan Ballubhai Madhyamic Shala, Maninagar*

The school was founded 75 years ago and is presently managed by a charitable trust. The school has a large, old building having many classrooms. A number of facilities are provided to the students and teachers. An open-air auditorium stands in one corner of the large playground. The school has audio-visual equipment too. There is a lot of stress on sports and physical education.

Four streams of education are offered to students at the Secondary level. Other than the usual streams of Science, Commerce and Arts, it offers technical course upto Class X. In its social context, it draws its students from all walks of life, as regards caste, religious, professional and socio-economic backgrounds. The total number of students is more than 1500. The school is co-educational in nature and the medium of instruction is Gujarati. The number of teachers is 50, besides the principal and vice-principal. The school has been identified as an innovative school which has played a pioneering role in introduction of innovations in the school system. Few of the innovations that call for mention are Gratuity Scheme for teachers, excursion, clubs and leadership training to students.

Allahabad (Uttar Pradesh)

3. *Kendriya Vidyalaya, Manauri*

The school is situated away from the city limits of Allahabad and in the vicinity of the Air Force Station. The school building is spacious with well laid out lawns and a garden. The classrooms are large having adequate furniture and proper furnishings. Physical facilities available are a library, toilets, drinking water, cycle stand and a gymnasium. The school offers only two streams — Science and Arts. Number of teachers in the higher secondary section stage are twelve, while the number of students is 150.

4. *D.P Girls' Inter College*

This is a privately managed institution housed in an old building. The space is inadequate as far as the number of students in the college is concerned. The physical facilities comprising of toilets, furniture, drinking water, cycle stand and library are also not sufficient. The classes are usually overcrowded.

The college offers two educational streams— Science and Arts. The Higher Secondary has ten sections of which six are those of Arts and four are Science sections. The students are admitted on the basis of merit. There are 763 students in the intermediate section, while the number of teachers in the same section is sixteen. The college gets grant-in-aid from the State Education Department. The medium of instruction is Hindi but the Science students are taught technical terms in English.

Bhubaneshwar (Orissa)

5. *Kendriya Vidyalaya No.1*

It is located near Utkal University in Bhubaneshwar. The students belong to varied backgrounds except for a small proportion of Oriya speaking students. The school building has a compound wall surrounding the campus. All essential physical facilities including adequately furnished classrooms are available in the school. The school also has a provision of audio-visual aids like the TV and projector. The total number of students in the school is 950 and the number of teachers is 46. The school offers only two streams of education, namely, Science and Arts.

6. *Demonstration Multipurpose School*

The school is situated in Mandhusudhannagar in west Bhubaneshwar. It is administered by the NCERT and has a local management committee under the Chairmanship of the Vice-Chancellor, Utkal

University. The examinations are conducted by the Central Board of Secondary Education.

The school has its own building with a compound wall. All classrooms are adequately equipped. Students are admitted after a written test. It offers two streams of education — Arts and Science. The total number of students in this school is 1145 and the number of teachers is 57.

Delhi (Union Territory)

7. *Andhra Education Society Senior Secondary School, Rouse Avenue*

It is situated near Tilak Bridge railway station surrounded by Central Government offices and other institutions. The school is managed by Andhra Education Society—a social-cultural association of Telugu speakers in Delhi. The management body is overall incharge for administration and management of the school. The school draws its students mainly from Andhra Pradesh. Being a Government aided school, 95 per cent of the finance comes as grant-in-aid from the Government.

The school comprises of two double-storeyed buildings in a very small area surrounded by a boundary wall. There is a small playground in between these two buildings. The school has library and laboratory facilities and a games room besides class rooms. The number of class rooms are fewer as compared to the student strength. The school offers all three streams of education—Science, Commerce and Arts. The Science stream has two sub-streams, namely, Biology and Engineering Drawing. The school follows the system of State Council of Education, Research and Training (SCERT) which is affiliated to the Central Board of Secondary Education. The school offers Telugu as its medium of instruction at the primary level while the medium of instruction is English at the secondary and senior secondary levels. Telugu is offered as an elective subject in the classes beyond primary level. The school also teaches photography, commercial art and painting as vocational and SUPW courses.

The number of students is nearly 2000 from primary to senior secondary level. The school is co-educational having more than 600 girls. Students are admitted on merit and performance in the entrance interview conducted for middle classes. The senior classes, however, do not have any such entrance test and admission is on the basis of marks in Class X. Some information sources quote that donations are also accepted by the school for admitting students.

8. *Government Girls' Higher Secondary School No. 2, Roop Nagar*

Located in a residential colony in Roop Nagar amidst thickly populated area, the school comes under the administration and management of Directorate of Education of Delhi Administration. It is under the jurisdicting of District North Educational Region of Delhi. SCERT attached to the Directorate of Education looks after some of the operational functions. It deals with the financial matters of the schools. It also acts as an advisory body in matters related to course, text books, teaching procedure and facilities, vocational course and SUPW activities.

The school has three buildings within a big enclosed compound having a big lawn and a playground. The school offers all three streams of education— Science, Commerce and Arts. Medium of instruction is Hindi except for Science stream in senior secondary level where it is English. Being a shared building, the school works in the morning session from 7 a.m to 12.30 p.m. The school draws its students mostly from the residential areas situated in its vicinity. The admission of students at middle and secondary levels is usually done on the basis of an entrance test. There are more than 2000 girls studying in this school from Class VI to Class XII. The number of teachers in the school, besides the principal, are 68. The school is one of the leading schools in Delhi as far as extra curricular activities are concerned. The students also have performed well at the Board examinations.

Guwahati (Assam)

9. *T.C. Government Girls' Higher Secondary and Multipurpose School, Uzanbuzur*

This Assamese medium Government school is situated in Uzanbazar— a fact growing commercial area which in the past was an Assamese "middle-class" residential area. The school is considered as the best Assamese medium girls' school in the city. All students are day scholars as there is no hostel facility.

The school is housed in an old, rather dilapidated, two-storeyed building built in Assamese style. The compound is frequently submerged in water during rainy season. However, a new brick building is being constructed within the school compound. The school has a large playground but there is little by way of day to day games and sports activities. There is acute scarcity of class room space and overcrowding in classes is a persistent problem for this school. Other essential physical facilities are adequate. The school does not have any audio-visual aids such as projector or television. The general up-keep and maintenance of the school are not at all satisfactory. Number of students in classes 5 to 12 is 1000 of which nearly 100 students are in higher secondary classes. The school offers only Arts and Science streams. Apart from the principal, there are 60 teachers in the school.

10. *Kendriya Vidyalaya, Khanapara*

The school, established in 1966, is situated on the southern fringe of the city, outside the Municipal Corporation boundary. The school is the oldest Central School in Guwahati. The school building is a one storeyed structure built in Assamese style. It has a large playground behind the building. Piped water supply is available. Other facilities include laboratories and library with a reading room. There are no audio-visual aids in this school.

The school is co-educational with both Hindi and English as medium of instruction. The school has nearly 1200 students from primary (Class I) to the higher secondary (Class XII) level. The higher secondary classes have about 100 students in all the three streams *i.e.* Science, Commerce and Arts. The number of teachers is 50 in this school. The students are all day scholars. They commute from the city by special school buses provided by the Assam State Road Transport Corporation.

Madras (Tamil Nadu)

11. *Kendriya Vidyalaya, Central Leather Research Institute, Adyar*

The school is located in front of the Indian Institute of Technology (IIT), Adyar. it has a double-storeyed building with modern architecture, beautiful lawn and playground. It has good library and laboratory facilities and enough class rooms that are well furnished. The school is rich in resources. Because of it being a project school, it gets all the funds whenever required from CLRI. The school is co-educational with English as medium of instruction. The number of students is above 1000 and the teachers are more than 50 in number.

12. *Corporation Girls' Higher Secondary School, Nungambakkam*

The girls' school, managed by Madras Municipal Corporation, is located in a slum area draws students mostly from families with a lower literacy level. The funds for innovative programmes are raised from the Corporation, which in terms of operation, is easier than interacting with State Government officials. But for educational rules and guidelines, it is governed by the Tamil Nadu State Board of Education.

The school building is good with a library and laboratories but the facilities are not above average. It offers all streams— Arts, Science and Commerce. The medium of instruction are both Tamil and English. Arts and Commerce are taught in Tamil whereas Science subjects are taught in English. It also offers vocational courses. The number of students is more than 1500 of which 220 are in Class XI itself.

The profile of twelve schools described in this chapter by and large shows that CLASS project schools were among the "better" schools having more than 1000 students on an average and adequate teaching staff. Infrastructure facilities like the school building, class rooms, laboratories and library were adequate in most of these schools. Two schools also mentioned having audio-visual aids. Of the 12, four schools were only for girls; the rest were co-educational, thereby, indicating adequate facilities of education for girls. All schools have Science and Arts streams of education while six also have Commerce.

While CLASS project schools cannot be described as special schools, the preponderance of Kendriya Vidyalayas changes to a certain extent the characteristics of a typical school. As computer learning was associated with Science, the selected CLASS schools were by and large having Science stream at the higher secondary level. All the twelve schools in this sample were having Science stream. This reflects that the sample drawn for the evaluation represents the universe of the study.

5

COMPUTER INSTALLATION AND COMPUTER TEACHER

Having described the general profile of 12 CLASS project schools, representing six states of the country, the attempt in this chapter will be to analyze the arrival of computer, its installation in schools, the computer teachers, their selection and training and perception about CLASS project. For the purpose of analysis, CLASS project schools can be divided into three categories, namely, State Government run, Kendriya Vidyalaya Sangathan, or NCERT and Privately managed or Trust schools as indicated in Chapter I.

Computer Installation

Available records indicate that by October-November 1984 the computers were available for installation in schools. Not all schools could get them installed immediately thus causing a delay of one month to a whole year. Table 5.1 gives information regarding the months when computers were installed and the period of delay in installation in six study cluster schools.

From the data received from 51 schools, it was observed that installation delays vary from 60 days to 360 days. There is a city-wise variation in installation delays. Installation of computers in the five schools of Guwahati was completed within three weeks of December 1984, whereas in Ahmedabad, Allahabad and Delhi, in some schools of Madras and Bhubaneshwar, installation was over within the first quarter of 1985. The remaining computers were installed in the second half of the year 1985. An exception to this is Madras, where the last two installations were completed on February 13, 1986. Reddy and Sujatha (1986:16) mentioned that, "the journey of computers to schools has not been swift or smooth. In fact, it is paradoxical that the symbols of latest technology should have moved like tortoises along a tortuous route. The complex formalities and protocols and the plurality of the agencies that deal with the same matter at different stages in ritualistically graced steps and a misunderstanding of the very nature and requirements of computer have all contributed to an inordinate delay in their installation and commissioning."

TABLE 5.1 : Period of Delay in Installation of Computers in Six Study Cluster Schools

Sr. No.	Name of the City	Months of Computer Installation	Delay in Installation of Computers (in months)
1.	Ahmedabad	November '84 to January '85	2 months
2.	Allahabad	January '85 to February '85	2-3 months
3.	Bhubaneshwar	February '85 to August '85	3-9 months
4.	Delhi	December '84 to January '85	1-2 months
5.	Guwahati	December '84	1 month
6.	Madras	December '84 to February '86	13 months

One tends to raise the question as to what were the factors responsible for the delay in the installation of computers which did not require very special preparation ? Some of the observed major factors for delay are discussed here. The explanation provided by the executing agency NCERT was that due to the assassination of the Prime Minister of India in October 1984 the whole project had a set-back leading to delays in the installation of the computers.

Lead Time

"The analysis shows that in every school after selection, it took some time for the renovation and electrification of the 'computer room'. Lack of funds may be a factor...as far as private schools were concerned. But... this was not the case in Kendriya Vidyalayas constituting about 40 per cent of the total CLASS project schools" (Agrawal, Sinha and Mullick 1986:26). Kendriya Vidyalayas faced problem of a different sort. To cite an example, the Kendriya Vidyalaya in Ahmedabad got delayed in the preparation of computer room due to wastage of time by Central Public Works Department (CPWD) people who had the responsibility of the renovation.. Most of the Kendriya Vidyalayas have to approach only the CPWD for any construction work. Hence, they had to depend on these engineers to get the job done. So, even in Kendriya Vidyalayas there was a need for lead time for the preparation of computer room. This lead time was reduced wherever the Resource Centres played an active role as in Guwahati and Delhi where their personnel visited the schools, helped in selection of room and installation of the computer. Two points emerge from the analysis :

1. There is need for clear recognition that a minimum of about 150 days of lead time was needed or required and this will increase further in the expansion phase because of factors such as geographical spread; and
2. The existence of Resource Centre or a similar agency would be essential in the installation phase and at a later stage for running the CLASS project smoothly. But, these must be active and should be able to interact with the schools at the working level.

Installation and Operation

There was in most cases, no delay between the arrival of the computer in the school and its installation. Exception apart, the computers were installed within a couple of days, after its arrival. In few cases, the delays were due to minor reasons like improper identification of the school or computer room. But there seems to be an appreciable time gap between what is technically known as "installation" according to CMC engineers and "operation" according to the computer teachers. The day a computer is brought in the school and connected to a plug, the computer is installed as per CMC engineers. But, according to computer teachers when it actually started working fully then it was operational. This variation in understanding has led to two different dates provided by the schools and CMC and Resource Centres. For example, in Madras, five out of nine computer schools reported delays of more than a month between installation and operation. Similar situations were observed in Bhubaneshwar and Allahabad. A clear definition of what constitutes "installation" should be worked out to minimize the conflict between the schools, the CMC engineers and Resource Centres.

Selection of Computer Teacher

During May 1984, the CLASS project schools received letters specifying the criteria for selection of teachers to be sent for training. The instructions in this regard in case of State Government and privately managed schools were given by the State Directorate of Education. Similar orders were issued for Kendriya Vidyalayas from Kendriya Vidyalaya Sangathan. These letters clearly stated that each CLASS project school should select at least three teachers and that these teachers should be Science or Commerce graduates. By the time these letters arrived in the schools, the school principals added another criterion—seniority as a basis for the selection of the computer teacher. So, majority of the teachers selected for CLASS project training were Science or Commerce graduates and were senior in the school.

As these letters were received during the summer vacation, those teachers available and fulfilling the selection criteria were selected without giving them any choice in the matter. Science teachers were mainly preferred as it was felt that being familiar to scientific instruments, they would find working on computers an easy job. Their science background would simplify the demystification process.

The principals selected senior teachers to avoid any charges of favouritism and they felt that given the charge of CLASS project to senior teachers would help in the smooth functioning of the project, as senior teachers would be able to exercise authority over their junior colleagues and students. As a result, the teachers from disciplines other than those specified were left out. Also, selecting senior teachers led to certain other problems. Some of these senior teachers were not interested in CLASS project which was not a positive sign at all. Some teachers were either transferred after undergoing training or were on the verge of retirement which meant that they could not contribute for long as computer teachers. Another side of the problem, as reported from one school in Madras, was that the younger teachers refused to take any initiative on their own lest it should offend the senior teacher. The teachers' disinterest led to withdrawal of many of them from CLASS project. There were a few who just refused to have anything to do with CLASS project after the training was over. Besides disinterest, other reasons for withdrawal were the feeling of extra burden and lack of any incentive.

The withdrawal of several computer teachers from CLASS project was observed. A number of reasons were given by these teachers. Important among these were extra burden, disinterest, no incentive and transfer. In Madras, eight of the computer teachers trained for CLASS project were utilized by the schools to conduct the Computer Science—elective/optional subject instead of CLASS project. The total number of withdrawals from CLASS project is quite high and needs considerable thought, as to the repercussion it might have had on the project.

Profile of the Computer Teacher

The profile of the computer teacher has been drawn from the data available from the holistic evaluation study. Among those selected as computer teachers there was a predominance of male teachers. Majority of the teachers belonged to the age group between 31 to 40 years, while a considerable number belonged to the higher age group of 41 to 50 years. Table 5.2 provides the gender-wise distribution of the computer teachers in the holistic evaluation study of schools.

TABLE 5.2 : Distribution of Computer Teachers By Gender

Sr. No.	Name of the City	Gender		Total
		Male	Female	
1.	Ahmedabad	78.9	21.1	100.0
2.	Allahabad	80.0	20.0	100.0
3.	Bhubaneshwar	90.0	10.0	100.0
4.	Delhi	61.4	38.6	100.0
5.	Guwahati	30.0	70.0	100.0
6.	Madras	78.3	21.7	100.0
	Percentage	68.4	31.6	100.0
	Sample	91	42	133

Table 5.2 shows the predominance of male teachers in all clusters except Guwahati where 70 per cent teachers were women. The teachers have been divided into two age groups, namely, 30 to 40 years and 41 to 50 years. The findings show that the number of teachers belonging to the age group 30 to 40 years is generally more than that belonging to the age group 41 to 50 years, though the difference is not really noticeable. This would mean a considerably large number

of teachers were in the higher age group and at a senior level in the school.

As mentioned earlier, Science teachers far outnumber Commerce and Arts teachers as computer teachers. Table 5.3 gives the percentage distribution of computer teachers by stream of education. As these teachers have to have masters degree for teaching in the higher secondary classes they were all master degree holders.

TABLE 5.3 : Distribution of Computer Teachers by Streams of Education

Sr. No.	Name of the City	Educational Streams			Total
		Science	Commerce	Arts	
1.	Ahmedabad	78.9	15.8	5.3	100.0
2.	Allahabad	90.0	10.0	–	100.0
3.	Bhubaneshwar	80.0	20.0	–	100.0
4.	Delhi	91.2	3.5	5.3	100.0
5.	Guwahati	100.0	–	–	100.0
6.	Madras*	73.9	26.1	–	100.0
	Percentage	86.0	10.9	3.1	100.0
	Sample	111	14	4	129

* Data on four teachers were not available.

What emerges as a computer teacher's profile fits very well with what was expected in the original guidelines provided for the selection of computer teachers. However, this portrayal is distinctly different from what one would expect to find in an average Higher Secondary School.

Training of Computer Teacher

On selection, as per instruction from NCERT, teachers were sent for a Basic Training Course of 21 days at the Resource Centres either in the same city or outside. The initial training programmes were conducted everywhere during the months of June and July 1984. As the time available to the schools for selection of teachers was limited, not all schools could arrange to send the required number of three teachers for the first Basic Training Course.

The course was an orientation to the computer teachers about the various capabilities and facilities available with a BBC microcomputer. The computer teachers were given theoretical instruction and practical demonstration-cum-hands-on practice on various packages that were to be part of the software for CLASS project.

The initial training programmes were satisfactorily undertaken in most of the cities. The picture that emerges from the training can be analysed from three sides, namely, the trainer (Resource Centre), trainee (the computer teacher) and the beneficiary (the student). Resource Centres at Madras and Baroda, where the first batch of computer teachers took training, received computers a week after the commencement of the training programme. This resulted in inadequate time for hands-on-practice for the computer teachers. Another reason for dissatisfaction was small number of computers available per computer teacher trainee. In Madras, there were seven computer terminals among 45 computer teachers. Similar problem recurred at other places also. The training programme at Madras was plagued with frequent power cuts which worsened the matters further.

The computer teachers were generally dissatisfied with the training. It could also be possible that their expectations from the training programme were at variance with the outcome. Most of the computer teachers expected to be taught about programming in BASIC which was just touched upon during the training programme and whatever taught was contrary to their expectations.

Advanced training courses in the summer of 1985 were held at Madras and Delhi, while at Ahmedabad, it had to be put off due to disturbances in the city. There was a year's gap between the Initial and the Advanced training courses at both places. Delhi Resource Centre did have a few orientation programmes and workshops in between. At Allahabad, the teachers were given a refresher course for two days just before the computers were installed. In general, it was observed that the teachers found the training inadequate. This tendency was well reflected in the knowledge level of computer teachers as a majority did not know about the CPU. As there was a large time gap between the training and start of the project, they were out of touch due to lack of practice. Some of them felt without the knowledge of programming, it was not possible for them to create any new programmes even if they wanted to. This in any way did not help promote the objectives of CLASS project.

Computer Teacher's Perception

The computer teachers had varied perceptions about a computer before they undertook training. Except for those few who had come into contact with computers earlier, most of the computer teachers had a vague idea about a computer. It was thought of as a super machine which was capable of solving any problem. Generally, computer teachers associated computers with programming. They were also not aware of its application in various areas. Training did provide them with an understanding of the functioning and applications of the computers in education besides other areas. Though it was felt that computers could be used as a teaching medium, a number of difficulties were pointed out by the computer teachers.

The first and foremost difficulty was regarding space—the computer rooms being small could not accommodate all the students of a class and the computer could not be taken to the regular class rooms. The computer teachers themselves also felt that they were not proficient enough and could not spare much time to prepare packages concerning their subjects. Lal and Joshi (1986) reported that in Ahmedabad computer teachers' perception of computers centred around training the students in programming to facilitate job opportunities for them. This perception was changed after the training and they realised that CLASS project was not a job oriented course at all but it was aimed towards spreading computer literacy.

During the initial stages of CLASS project, a majority of the computer teachers felt happy and proud to be associated with computers. At Delhi, many of the teachers were under the impression that it would be introduced as an optional subject while the Ahmedabad teachers felt that this was a job oriented course. However, once the computers were installed and the project took off, the increasing workload and other problems connected with it dampened the enthusiasm of the computer teachers. The computer teachers at Delhi and Ahmedabad found their first impression of a computer not coinciding with what they experienced later on.

The feeling that CLASS project was an extera work load for the computer teachers who could not relief from the regular work they had been hitherto performing, was common everywhere. It was felt that some incentive, either monetary in form of honorarium or reduction of the normal workload of the computer teachers, would positively help. Another suggestion was to appoint a full time computer teacher who could look after all the affairs of the project. Keeping this suggestion in view, in one of the schools in Ahmedabad the computer teacher was made computer incharge and was relieved from other teaching responsibilities.

The teachers felt that the arrangement of computer classes should be within the school hours and adjusted in the school time table. Kendriya Vidyalaya teachers suggested that there should be a specific directive from Kendriya Vidyalaya Sangathan regarding the arrangement of computer classes and the Socially Useful and Productive Work (SUPW) periods. Kendriya Vidyalaya teachers also felt that CLASS project got lower priority compared to the regular subjects as it was not an examination subject. Kendriya Vidyalayas, in trying to get a good result in their regular subjects, tended to sideline CLASS project.

The computer teachers faced a main problem of inadequate training and a large time gap between training and actual computer use. As a result, the computer teachers were not adequately equipped to handle a class of students where the students would ask so many questions. At some places, the teachers had problems amongst themselves. Mahapatra and Swain (1986) in Bhubaneshwar and Bhandari (1986) in Delhi reported incidents where the incharge to the computer room did not allow free access of the other computer teachers to the computer room. Interpersonal problems amongst the computer teachers also adversely affected the functioning of CLASS project.

Demystification of Non-computer Teachers

Schools have always played an important role as centres for dissemination of information. The CLASS project, which represents a vital innovation in recent years, is expected to generate its own centrifugal impact on the wider community. Hence, any study of the CLASS project should focus some attention on the processes of the percolation of computer awareness from the school to the neighbourhood, from the students to their parents and their friends and from the teachers to the larger society.

Within the school itself, there is diffusion of information about the computers from the computer teachers and computer students—who are at the giving end—to the non-computer teachers and non-computer students—who are at the receiving end.

The Madras report states that during the initial stages of the CLASS project there were quite a few non-computer teachers who were unhappy over their not being chosen for computer training. But, with the passage of time, they felt only too happy to be saved from the problems which the computer teachers had to face. Though some teachers were positively inclined towards computer learning, they were at the same time apprehensive of the additional work load it would entail without bringing them any compensatory benefits. This was true for other computer schools also. The access of non-computer teachers to the computer room depended on their personal inclination, interest and relationship with the computer teachers. Their level of awareness was not very high. Many of the non-computer teachers felt that computer class was a waste of time as it did not teach anything constructive and took up time of other subjects. They felt that the computer teachers required proper training.

Views of the Computer Teachers on Adequacy of CLASS Project

In general, the computer teachers appeared to be confused about the aims of CLASS project and its place in the school curriculum. Although they valued the objectives of computer awareness and literacy, they were skeptical about the adequacy of the CLASS project in the present form and felt that much more needed to be done to improve the scope of the project. The computer teachers opined that merely learning to operate the computer with a readymade software package may not really be purposeful. Hence, programming in BASIC should be taught to the students systematically. But, the computer teachers hastened to express their own deficiency of training in this regard. Most of them asked for regular refresher courses in computer training. But, on the other hand, they felt that if they learnt more they would have to teach more which would only be inviting more trouble for themselves. In Madras, majority of the teachers thought that the computer can be utilized, ideally speaking, as an aid to teaching of regular subjects. However, from the practical point of view, they too expresses the difficulty in using the computer for this purpose. Yet, if the computer is to be used as teaching aid, it would be necessary to have many more software packages for each subject. As things stand, the software packages supplied were too few and not interesting enough to engage the attention of students over a full academic year.

The CLASS project remained outside both the curricular and the co-curricular regimen. So, the computer teachers found it unreasonable to compel the students to learn computer operations when they should be concentrating on the curricular subjects. The computer teachers themselves become lax towards the project for the same reason. It may be mentioned here that the computer teachers felt that the CLASS project in its present form may be more suited to lower classes from VI to IXth. They strongly suggested that a non-examination-oriented activity should not receive much time and attention in higher classes such as X, XI or XIIth standards, when the students should spend more of their time in preparing for the examinations.

A minority among the computer teachers felt strongly against any kind of computer education in schools. These teachers felt that it is more essential to impart basic knowledge in different subjects to students than let them play with computers. Investing in computers was considered by them to be a waste of resources which can better be diverted into more purposeful avenues like supplying books, notebooks and other stationary to poor children or equipping the schools with some basic amenities which were lacking.

For the success of CLASS project, the teachers recommended a clear working syllabus. Selection of teachers called for more attention. It was felt that teachers on the verge of retirement should not be selected as computer teachers. Some of the teachers felt that the software should be in a local language which would make it easier for the students to understand what they were doing. The interaction between Resource Centre and schools had to be more frequent if the project was to function smoothly. Finally, introducing computer education only in a few city schools would not be helpful as it would not cover the entire student population in India.

6

THE STUDENTS AND COMPUTER DEMYSTIFICATION
A Qualitative Analysis

So far, two vital aspects of the CLASS project, namely, computer installation and computer teachers have been examined. One of the most important objective of the CLASS project was to demystify students about computer. This chapter provides qualitative understanding of the extent to which the demystification took place and the factors, if any, hindered the process of demystification.

The CLASS project was introduced for students of Class XI studying in various educational systems as discussed in Chapter I. In some states and in Kendriya Vidyalayas, Class XI is a part of Higher Secondary schools, whereas in other places it falls under intermediate or junior college, though there is an effort to have an uniform 10 + 2 higher secondary system throughout the country. This distinction has been made earlier but it is repeated here to bring out the subtle attitudinal differences towards computer among the students studying in different systems. It is vividly exemplified in Assam and Orissa where admission in higher secondary for Class XI is considered inferior when compared to Class XI admission in the college. Therefore, bright students prefer to go to college rather than higher secondary school.

Profile of Computer Learners

On the criteria to be adopted for selecting students for the course, the understanding evolved was that the programme should not be limited only to academically advanced students. A mixed group would enable the teacher and the school to assess the role of the micro-computer in enhancing self-learning ability of students with widely differing competency. The rationale for restricting CLASS project to higher secondary students for the time being was that "the students output would go into the national work force much sooner than the children in the primary schools... Besides, it would be more manageable ..." at the plus two stage... "in the beginning and with experience gained at this stage, it would be possible to implement computer education programme on a wider scale at the primary level subsequently" (Report of the National Workshop on Computer Literacy Curriculum held at NCERT on 26-27 March, 1984:70-71).

Generally, students from Science stream seemed to hold immediate preference over students from other streams for computer learning. It is obvious from the enrollment figures collected from 42 schools. The analysis shows that more than 75 per cent of the students for CLASS project were selected from Science stream. In Delhi alone, 512 out of 626 students were from Science stream. Similar figures were obtained in the other computer schools. The exception was Ahmedabad, where along with Science, Commerce students were also selected in a large number (Science 115 and Commerce 95). Table 6.1 gives the distribution of students in the three streams of education collected from the schools studied as a part of holistic evaluation.

TABLE 6.1 : Distribution of Students by Educational Stream

Sr. No.	Name of the City	Educational Streams			
		Science	Commerce	Arts	Total
1.	Ahmedabad	115	95	33	243
2.	Allahabad	105	15	17	137
3.	Bhubaneshwar	108	24	7	139
4.	Delhi	512	84	30	626
5.	Guwahati	204	–	4	208
6.	Madras	148	40	40	248
	Total	1192	258	131	1581
	Percentage	75.4	16.3	8.3	100.0

The initial bias favouring Science students can be attributed to the majority of Science teachers amongst the computer teachers. Besides, the computer was perceived as being closely related to Science and, therefore, was thought to be suitable for science students who may be better equipped to learn computer. Also, Science students generally are academically high achievers. Hence, it is clear that the students selected for CLASS project were among the best achievers.

Although "objective" criterias were developed by each computer teacher or school ranging from "test", "interviews" and "merit", in the final selection, it was the Science students who dominated the CLASS project. Certain CLASS project schools made it compulsory for all the students of a particular class or section to enroll in the computer class. The explanation provided for the same was that this procedure was less time consuming and complaints regarding favouritism could be avoided. Better class grade and knowledge of English or typing were also considered as criteria for selection of students in some CLASS project schools. Irrespective of the criteria developed by the schools, a need was felt for developing new and uniform methods of selection of students for broader spread of computer literacy.

The computer students' personal attributes are closely linked with their social attributes. Most of the selected students belonged to a small family of four to five members. The educational and economic background of parents provided a clue to understand the students' socio-economic status. Table 6.2 and 6.3 present the educational and economic status of parents of computer students from the selected CLASS project schools. Exceptions apart, almost all parents are educated that too majority being bachelors and master's degree holders (Table 6.2). Their median monthly income is between Rs. 2500-5000 (Table 6.3). Thus, socio-economic status of the computer students are relatively higher as compared to average socio-economic status of other students.

Further analysis showed that the educational level of the parents and economic status of students from Kendriya Vidyalayas was generally higher than those from other schools in the city area. Also, the student population of Kendriya Vidyalayas was from a varied educational, economic and cultural background.

Learning Environment and Computer Exposure

While there was no disagreement that computer must be taught and utilized by the students, there seemed to be many hurdles in doing so. Variations in the individual teacher's attitude towards CLASS project; problem of scheduling the computer class; pressure of conflicting interest, especially of examination and results; management and principals, attitude towards computer classes; all these affected the computer learning environment of the school.

TABLE 6.2 : Distribution of Parents of Computer Students by Education Level

Sr. No.	Name of the City	Education Level							Total
		Illiterate	Primary	Secondary	Higher Secondary	Graduate	Post-Graduate	No Response	
1.	Ahmedabad	–	1	6	1	37	34	3	82
2.	Delhi	–	–	7	30	24	18	–	79
3.	Guwahati	2	–	6	10	25	11	–	54
4.	Madras	–	4	25	–	10	21	–	60
	Total	2	5	44	41	96	84	3	275
	Percentage	0.7	1.8	16.0	14.9	34.9	30.6	1.1	100.0

Note : Data from Bhubaneshwar and Allahabad not reported.

TABLE 6.3 : Distribution of Parents of Computer Students by Monthly Income

Sr. No.	Name of the City	Income					Total
		Below Rs. 1000	Rs. 1000 to Rs. 2500	Rs. 2500 to Rs. 5000	Rs. 5000 and above	N.R.	
1.	Ahmedabad	3	37	16	–	26	82
2.	Allahabad	–	16	50	–	–	66
3.	Delhi	1	19	26	2	31	79
4.	Madras	32	6	22	–	–	60
	Total	36	78	114	2	57	287
	Percentage	12.5	27.2	39.7	0.7	19.9	100.0

Note : Data from Bhubaneshwar and Guwahati not reported.

As indicated in Chapter I, the guideline provided 30 hours of theory and 60 hours of practical spread over 30 weeks in the first year of CLASS project. Such a duration of exposure was considered necessary for individual or group hands-on-practice for an effective utilization of the software. It was felt that each student in a group of three to four should have access to a computer terminal at least once in a week for one full period. The CLASS project schools were expected to rearrange their time table for the students selected from a given class in such a way that those students who opt for computer literacy were relieved from attending classes like SUPW, work experience, games and library work.

None of the 51 schools studied could provide 30 hours of theory and 60 hours of practicals to the computer students. It is important to note that there were only two computer terminals for practicals, thereby limiting the "operational time" for each student. First of all, there was no clear demarcation between theory-cum-demonstration and practical classes as indicated in Guwahati. Most of the computer sessions began with theory and demonstration by the computer teachers, followed by practice session for the students. Secondly, the total computer time varied from zero exposure to as low as an exposure time of seven hours in a year in Guwahati and to as high as 35 hours in a year in Madras. The analysis shows that the CLASS project was a non-starter in one school at least in each study cluster of the 51 schools.

On an average, 38 students were selected for computer class in each school. But the variation was very high, the lowest being 11 in a school in Guwahati and the highest being 120 in a Madras school. The larger the number of computer students, lesser was the time for hands-on practice. In each of the CLASS project schools, the computer students were divided into groups and each of the three computer teachers was expected to take care of a few batches. The number of computer students per batch also varied but was generally six to ten students per batch. The number of batches increased with the number of computer students. Each batch would attend a computer class in rotation. This meant that if the number of batches was large, it would take longer time for each batch to attend the subsequent computer class. Non-participation of a few computer teachers in the initial computer training also resulted in large batch formation and crowding in the computer room. A batch of 20 students could use two computer terminals once in a month or maximum twice in a month.

Three problems emerged from such an arrangement—one, crowding in the computer room and two, long intervals between computer classes. The computer students were, therefore, unable to retain the new information given to them. The computer time per student also worked out to be five to ten minutes per computer class in schools that had selected a large number of computer students. Third problem observed relates to small group dynamics of learning, in which boys tried to dominate girls in the class and took their hands-on-practical time away or strong and smart boys forced weak boys to relinquish their turns in their favour. The whole computer room dynamics is described in the following words :

> "Students are all uniformly enthusiastic in handling the computer. This can be seen obviously from the manner in which the students rush from their class room to the computer room and vie with each other to enter the room first in order to be the first to handle the keyboard. Here again, differing patterns of behavior could be noticed between girls and boys. While to a large extent, there was orderliness amongst the girls, the boys continued to be disorderly even towards the end of the academic year. After the first few classes, the girls quite seriously worked out amongst themselves for how much time each one of them would handle the computer and followed that norm, each one taking her turn. Out-of-the-turn handling by a girl occurred only when the teacher would ask some students, whom she considered to be good, to work on the software, asking the other students to answer some pertinent questions and observed the monitor. Among the boys, often a strong-willed person elbows out other, resulting in some commotion and quarelling at the beginning of every class. Invariably, it was the teacher who would step in and decide as to which student will handle the keyboard first. However, both among the boys and girls, there were a few students who were shy and not very confident of themselves until the end. These few pupils would generally relinquish their turn to others after initially punching a few key." (Reddy and Sujatha 1986:124).

The problem of sharing computer time occurred usually where the number of students per computer was large resulting in dissatisfaction among students regarding the computer time available to them. Also, the presence of computer teachers in the computer room made a lot of difference, as they could see to it that everybody got their turn. Many students considered computer classes as "recreation time" when they could for a little while get away from their classrooms.

Aspirations and Perceptions of Students

The students generally were happy to work on the computer. Most of them took it to be an exciting prospect. Kendriya Vidyalaya students were generally found to be better informed about a computer and its applications when compared to students from State Government or private schools. Many students of schools other than Kendriya Vidyalayas were also knowledgeable about a computer before enrolling for CLASS project. That information could be due to the educational background of their families and their access to relevant reading material. Most of the students discussed about their experiences in the computer class at home. Enrolling for CLASS project was for some students a preparatory phase for a career in the field of computer.

Generally, computer evoked considerable interest among the students during the initial period. But, this enthusiasm gradually waned with the passage of time. This could be attributed to a number of reasons. Important among these were few computer classes and insufficient time for hands-on-practice. Students from schools, where teachers had been lax in providing guidance, were a dissatisfied lot. All computer schools in Guwahati except one did not have scheduled class for computer learning which resulted in a chaotic situation for students who did not know when the next class would be held. A similar problem was reported from Kendriya Vidyalaya, Ahmedabad also where the classes were very irregularly held. Most students felt that there should be no compulsion on any student to join computer class if not interested. The software packages supplied for CLASS project were found uninteresting by the Ahmedabad Kendriya Vidyalaya students. The Gujarati medium students in Ahmedabad schools used software packages to learn English. It was generally observed that sustenance of student interest was to a large extent dependent on the method of instruction followed by the computer teachers. Lackadaisical attitude of school authorities led to disillusionment about computers among students, thus, bringing about a loss of interest in attending the computer class. This is a serious matter for computer education planners to consider. A way must be found out to tackle this situation.

Demystification Process

The goal of computer demystification was not achieved. Out of 51 CLASS project schools, in six CLASS project schools no computer classes were held. In the remaining 45 schools, varying degrees of computer learning took place. Even after the end of the second year of the project, in April 1986, it was observed that computer students were unable to load a floppy after eight months of training in one of the CLASS project schools. On the other hand, in a Kendriya Vidyalaya of Bhubaneshwar, few students were observed helping the computer teacher to prepare annual progress report of the students on BBC computer.

It would be difficult to quantify the degree of demystification, but observations made it amply clear that out of some 1500 students, only a few were demystified, although a large number of them were aware about computer. In Allahabad, it was observed that the computer students of five schools knew what a computer looked like. They were able to identify the keyboard, floppy and monitor. But none of the students could ascertain the location of the Central Processing Unit (CPU), though they were aware of the function carried out by the CPU. The different input and output devices of a computer were not known to most of the computer students. Proficiency in keyboard operation was lacking amongst almost all the computer students. The computer students had a vague understanding about the role of computer in education and other walks of life. In short, a very limited awareness about the computer, its components and applications was found among the computer students in spite of one year of computer exposure.

A similar observation was made in Ahmedabad, where language difficulty compounded the problem. In Bhubaneshwar, lack of knowledge of English language become a barrier for computer demystification, apart from low computer exposure. In one of the Delhi schools, the computer students during the year's time had attended 8 to 10 classes only and had just operated two software packages. Their knowledge about computer and its functions was also very low. In Guwahati, due to irregular and infrequent classes, CLASS project had an inadequate and uneven impact on the students. In Madras, it was observed that the demystification of a computer was at the maximum among the students who were able to handle computer by themselves. But then, most of them were unable to do so. In none of the CLASS project schools, did the students get the required training or time to gain familiarity and competence in the use of computer.

On the whole, the level of demystification was found to be very low. The main reason being that few computer classes than prescribed were held which was as low as a single computer class, thereby reducing the positive impact of learning. Understanding of English language, the medium of computer teaching in some schools, was a problem and most important of all, many of the teachers themselves were not demystified.

Two points that have emerged from the analysis are that students were keen to learn computer and they were capable of learning and mastering the computer. However, there was little computer exposure to the students due to several factors indicated earlier in the chapter. The most important recommendation is that all efforts be made to see that the students get hands-on-practice as originally recommended in order to demystify them. Also, the stringent selection criteria adopted by the schools favour Science students. Therefore, efforts are required to find ways and means to have the benefit of computer literacy spread over a large section of the student community, so that the benefit is shared equally.

Demystification of Non-Computer Students

The non-computer students seemed to be very much interested in learning computer. Most of them were sore about being left out. The non-computer students generally did not have much access to the computer room besides a few curious and interested ones who managed to have a peep inside once in a while. The information dissemination process seemed to be a very slow one as not much information gain was observed among these students. The non-computer students studying in the Arts stream in Kendriya Vidyalaya, Ahmedabad, felt that computers would not help them in their future education or career. So, they were glad that they were not forced to enroll in the CLASS project as their other classmates studying in Science and Arts streams were made to do. Barring these few, most of the non-computer students evinced keen interest in attending computer classes if given the opportunity. Computers seemed to have caught the imagination of each and everyone in the school campus whether or not directly associated with it.

The dissemination of information outside the school campus was not much. The students did talk about their classroom experiences at home but the parents did not seem to know what exactly their child did in the computer class at school. They felt that knowledge of programming was essential for the students enrolled in a computer class. None of the schools really made any effort to make the parents aware about CLASS project, its aims and objectives. An effort in this direction could be useful.

7

THE STUDENTS AND COMPUTER DEMYSTIFICATION
A Quantitative Analysis

In this chapter, an attempt will be made to measure the computer demystification of students through survey data. In order to do so, first the socio-economic status of the computer students from about 10 per cent of the total schools under CLASS project will be analyzed.

The Socio-Economic Profile of Computer Students

There are 54 per cent boys and 46 per cent girls in the sample which is not what one would find at the higher secondary level in the country (see Table 7.1). The reason is that there was a conscious effort to have a fair representation of both genders in the sample for comparison in the survey. However, it may be mentioned that ratio of boys and girls at the higher secondary level in the country is more skewed in favour of boys. Most of these students are sixteen or seventeen years of age. It was observed that Kendriya Vidyalaya students are slightly older than those in State Government run schools. This is because of the differing admission ages to the first grade in these two types of

TABLE 7.1 : Distribution of Students by Gender and School Management

Sr. No.	*School Management*	*Boys*	*Girls*	*Total*
1.	Kendriya Vidyalaya	60.8	39.2	100
2.	State Government	39.1	60.9	100
3.	State aided/Private	64.3	35.7	100
	Average	53.7	46.3	100
	Sample	292	252	544

schools.

Table 7.2 shows that barring a small percentage of students studying in high schools (11.0 per cent), more than three-fourth of the students selected for CLASS project are from Classes XI and XII. It may be mentioned that 41 per cent of the students of Kendriya Vidyalayas are from Class XII. It is because by the time they filled the questionnaire they had been promoted to Class XII in April 1986

TABLE 7.2 : Distribution of Students by Class and School Management

Sr. No.	School Management	Class				
		IX and Below IX*	X	XI	XII	Total
1.	Kendriya Vidyalaya	7.1	1.1	51.1	40.7	100.0 (268)
2.	State Government	10.9	34.8	45.8	8.4	100.0 (192)
3.	State aided/ Private	23.8	0.0	64.3	11.9	100.0 (84)
	Average Sample**	11.0	12.9	51.3	24.8	100.0 (544)

* There were not more than one per cent students in below Class IX so they have been merged with Class IX.

** Sample size is given in parenthesis.

during the survey, which is not the case in State schools.

Similarly, further analysis of Table 7.2 shows that out of 23.9 per cent of computer students of Class IX and X more than two-third of them are from the State run schools. This is because computers were supplied to State run High Schools and not Intermediate/Junior Colleges where XI and XII Classes are held in those States. It is significant to point out that almost three-fourth of the students who are considered "better students" are from the Science stream, as science students with mathematics were selected by the computer teachers for CLASS project.

Table 7.3 shows that the occupation of majority (51.5 per cent) of the father/guardians of the computer students is managerial. However, there is a distinct difference between computer students of Kendriya Vidyalayas, State Government run and State aided schools. While the occupation of 68.7 per cent of the fathers is managerial in the Kendriya Vidyalayas, not more than 37.5 per cent of fathers of State Government school computer students fall in this category. This reflects the fact that majority of Kendriya Vidyalaya students are from higher income groups, while a majority of students studying in the State Government and State Government aided schools come from middle income families having white collar jobs. It also shows that very few children of blue collar workers are able to make it to the higher secondary level of education. In this respect the sample represents the socio-economic profile of those students who come from the educated upper crust of society; whose family expenditure is many times more than the average per-capita expenditure in the country.

TABLE 7.3 : Distribution of Students' Fathers' Occupation by School Management

Sr. No.	School Management	Managerial Job 1	White Collar Job 2	Blue Collar Job 3	No Reply	Total
1.	Kendriya Vidyalaya	68.7	28.3	1.1	1.9	100.0 (268)
2.	State Government	37.5	44.8	15.1	2.6	100.0 (192)
3.	State aided/ Private	28.6	56.0	9.5	5.9	100.0 (84)
	Average Sample	51.5	38.4	7.3	2.8	100.0 (544)

Sample size is given in parenthesis.

1. Managerial Job : Engineer, Doctor, IAS, Lawyer, Manager, Military Officer, Professor, Big Businessman, Large Industry Owner and Large Farmer.
2. White Collar Job: Clerk, Stenographer, Teacher, Compounder, Supervisor, Foreman, Accountant, Draughtsman, Medium Level Businessman, Medium Level Industry Owner, Medium Level Farmer.
3. Blue Collar Job: Driver, Conductor, Peon, Factory Worker, Watchman, Mechanic, Gardener, Small Businessman, Cottage Industry Owner, Small Farmer, Daily Wage Worker.

Awareness of CLASS Project

Exceptions apart, the computer students surveyed were aware of the existence of the CLASS project. General observations show that this is true for almost all the schools. Table 7.4 shows that there are no significant differences between the Kendriya Vidyalayas and State run schools in the level of awareness about CLASS project among computer students. It is important to note that most of the Class XI and XII students, who participated in CLASS project, were those who were studying in the school before computers were installed in the first quarter of 1985. It may, therefore, be interpreted that there was a low visibility of CLASS project in the schools.

TABLE 7.4 : Distribution of Awareness among Students about CLASS Project by School Management

Sr. No.	School Management	Aware	Not Aware	No Reply	Total
1.	Kendriya Vidyalaya	97.0	2.0	1.0	100.0 (268)
2.	State Government	97.9	1.6	0.5	100.0 (192)
3.	State aided/Private	94.0	1.2	4.8	100.0 (84)
	Average Sample	96.9	1.7	1.4	100.0 (544)

Sample size is given in parenthesis.

Computer Utilization

Before analysing the computer utilization by the students, it is necessary to calculate the average number of hours the students participated in both theory and practical classes. For computer demystification 30 hours of theory and 60 hours of practical classes during an academic year were recommended by the National Workshop on the Computer Literacy (1984). Various observations and estimates have brought out that very little distinction was made by the computer teachers between theory and practical classes. Actually, in most cases, they were combined, with the first few minutes devoted to "theory" and demonstration followed by "practical". It is, therefor, difficult to separate the two kinds of classes. On an average, the computer students got four hours and forty minutes in a month to work on computer (see Table 7.5).

However, this is a misleading average calculation, as there is a wide variation, beginning from no computer hands-on-practice to 50 hours indicated by few students in the CLASS project where computer functioning was reported to be irregular. Table 7.5 shows that on an average 5 hours 16 minutes per month were spent in computer teaching according to the teachers, where the Kendriya Vidyalayas computer teacher spent the highest time (6 hours and 16 minutes), and the State Government run schools spent the lowest time (3 hours and 18 minutes). The average hours spent on computer learning per month, as indicated by computer students is no different than that by the computer teachers (see Table 7.5) but the computer teachers, it seems, have over reported in all categories.

TABLE 7.5 : Average of Computer Classes Held According to Students and Teachers in a Month by Periods and Hours by School Management

Sr. No.	School Management	According to Students: Average in Hours and Minutes	According to Teachers: Average in Periods	According to Teachers: Average in Hours and Minutes
1.	Kendriya Vidyalaya	4'10"	10.75	6'16"
2.	State Government	5'49"	4.96	3'18"
3.	State Aided/Private	3'45"	7.07	4'43"
	Average	4'40"	8.46	5'16"

* In Kendriya Vidyalayas, periods were calculated on the basis of 35 minutes per period and in State Government run and State aided schools it was 40 minutes per period.

Table 7.6 shows that 88.4 per cent computer students used the computer in a group situation. Only about 7.4 per cent were able to use it individually. Table 7.6 further shows that this pattern was

TABLE 7.6 : Distribution of Computer Operation by School Management

Sr. No.	School Management	Individually	In Groups	No Reply	Total
1.	Kendriya Vidyalaya	9.0	88.4	2.6	100.0 (268)
2.	State Government	4.7	89.6	5.7	100.0 (192)
3.	State Aided/Private	8.3	85.7	6.0	100.0 (84)
	Average Sample	7.4	88.4	4.2	100.0 (544)

Sample size is given in parenthesis

TABLE 7.7 : Distribution of Attention Given by Teachers to Computer Students by School Management

Sr. No.	School Management	Fast Learner	Slow Learner	No Reply	Total
1.	Kendriya Vidyalaya	41.0	39.9	19.1	100.0 (268)
2.	State Government	52.1	41.7	6.2	100.0 (192)
3.	State Aided/Private	52.4	48.8	4.8	100.0 (84)
	Average Sample	46.7	48.8	12.3	100.0 (544)

Sample size is given in parenthesis.

consistent for each category schools. It was observed that dominating students were able to use the computer longer than the others. Hence, there was an uneven hands-on experience for the computer students. The computer teachers' attitude was to provide help to "fast learners" as indicated in Table 7.7. Table 7.7 shows that 46.7 per cent computer students felt that teachers gave more attention to fast learners. This kind of feeling was strongly expressed by the computer students of State Government and Government aided schools rather than Kendriya Vidyalayas. One possible explanation could be that heterogeneity of the student population in Kendriya Vidyalayas does not permit such partial treatment, or that the average students of this kind of school is better than those of State run school. But it must be pointed out that the opinion on this question are more or less equally divided.

It seems that computer learning has created some excitement among the computer students who feel like discussing computer experiences with their near and dear. Table 7.8 shows that seven computer students out of ten have discussed about computer with their friends in and outside the school. The parents are ranked second, followed by siblings. Non-computer students and neighbours are ranked fourth and fifth respectively. It was observed that the computer students also acted as agents for information dissemination about computer. Further analysis shows that more than three-fourth of the computer students (77 per cent) wanted to learn computer in the school whereas only 20 per cent preferred to go to a private institution for learning computer. Only three per cent would not like to learn computer beyond whatever they have learnt so far. There is no

TABLE 7.8 : Distribution of Information Dissemination by Computer Students

Sr. No.	Information Dissemination	Yes	No	Rank	Total
1.	To parents	63.9	36.1	II	100.0 (544)
2.	To sisters and brothers	49.2	50.8	III	100.0 (544)
3.	To friends	70.2	29.8	I	100.0 (544)
4.	To neighbours	26.8	73.2	V	100.0 (544)
5.	To non-computer students	36.3	63.7	IV	100.0 (544)
6.	Others	7.4	92.6	VI	100.0 (544)

Sample size is given in parenthesis.

variation in this response among students coming from different kinds of schools. One may interpret this finding as a positive indication for the introduction of computer in the school education as one of the subjects.

Having analyzed the students' socio-economic characteristics, their preferences for learning computer, we now turn our attention to their level of computer demystification.

Computer Demystification

The operational definition of computer demystification included several indicators which were agreed by the computer experts as operationally defined in Chapter 3. Accordingly, 15 knowledge items of equal weightage were selected for measuring computer demystification. A "demystified" student was the one who could score 11 points on the knowledge scale of 15 points containing 15 items. Anyone, who scored minimum of six points on a 15 points knowledge scale, was considered "partially demystified". Those who scored below five points were considered "not demystified". Ideally anyone getting less than 15 points should be considered not or partially demystified. But given the novelty of the educational technology like computer, after considerable debate equal interval categories were made to measure demystification. Table 7.9 shows that 15.6 per cent computer students got demystified as a result of CLASS project. Another 33.1

per cent got partially demystified and the remaining 51.3 remained not deymstified. Further, Table 7.9 shows that there is a gradual decrease in the level of deymstification from Kendriya Vidyalayas (19.6 per cent) to State aided/private schools (1.2 per cent). State Government run schools fall in the middle having 16.7 per cent demystified. The same trend has been observed in the case of partially demystified, but the difference is not as sharp as in the case of demystified students, where 71.4 per cent students belong to State aided or private schools. The explanation for these differences lie in the exposure of computer as indicated in Table 7.5 where State aided/private schools have shown spending comparatively fewer period on computer literacy.

It is a safe hunch that if the computer students were given 90 hours of training, majority of them would have been demystified. This is fairly evident from the Table 7.10 which shows that the non-computer students of the same school were demystified by 1.4 per cent and 92.5 per cent remained mystified. This small percentage of demystified students much be those who made their way to computer rooms, as it has been observed that students not selected for computer classes, tried to learn computers with the help of their peers in the school.

TABLE 7.9 : Distribution of Computer Students Demystified by School Management

Sr. No.	School Management	Not Demysti-fied	Partially Demysti-fied	Demy-stified	Total
1.	Kendriya Vidyalaya	45.1	35.3	19.6	100.0 (268)
2.	State Govt. School	50.5	32.8	16.7	100.0 (192)
3.	State Aided/Private School	71.4	27.4	1.2	100.0 (84)
	Average Sample	51.3	33.1	15.6	100.0 (544)

Sample size is given in parenthesis.

Initial observations indicated that in almost all CLASS project schools, 'WELCOME' package was most widely used and was the most popular package amongst students. Accordingly, it was thought most appropriate to evaluate, as a part of demystification, the computer operation ability of the student by testing to what extent, they had

TABLE 7.10 : Distribution of Non-Computer Students Demystified by School Management

Sr. No.	School Management	Not Demystified	Partially Demystified	Demystified	Total
1.	Kendriya Vidyalaya	90.6	7.2	2.2	100.0 (181)
2.	State Government	95.9	3.1	1.0	100.0 (222)
3.	State Aided/Private School	88.8	10.3	0.9	100.0 (107)
	Average Sample	92.5	6.1	1.4	100.0 (510)

Sample size is given in parenthesis.

learnt correct steps to be followed for using 'WELCOME' package. A test of five items was prepared accordingly. Table 7.11 shows that 57.0 per cent students can indicate the correct steps to be followed for WELCOME package. Of course, there are variations among Kendriya Vidyalayas and State Government and State aided schools. This analysis further reaffirms that, if appropriate exposure is given to the students they will get demystified.

TABLE 7.11 : Distribution of Students Knowing Correct Steps to be Followed to Use 'WELCOME' Package

Sr. No.	*School Management*	*Knows*	*Does not know*	*Total*
1.	Kendriya Vidyalaya	63.1	36.9	100.0 (268)
2.	State Government	49.0	51.0	100.0 (192)
3.	State Aided/Private School	56.0	44.0	100.0 (84)
	Average Sample	57.0	43.0	100.0 (544)

Sample size is given in parenthesis.

In this survey, the effort has been to measure the extent of computer demystification that has occurred as a result of CLASS project. The results are clearly indicative of marginal gains, as not more than 15 per cent students have got demystified in the academic year of 1985-86. To have 100 per cent demystification, a full programme of 90 hours seems to be essential. This requires rigorous changes in the programme. Efforts are required to provide better scheduling of computer classes in the school time-table, incentives to computer teachers and involvement of various educational functionaries, both at the state and district levels.

8

MANAGEMENT OF CLASS PROJECT

So far, we have analyzed the extent of demystification of computer. Both qualitative and quantitative analyses have clearly indicated that while there was no difficulty in learning computer on the part of the students, the demystification was very low. In order to understand the antecedents of low demystification, it was felt essential to probe into factors related to CLASS project management. In this chapter the factors related to management of the CLASS project will be analyzed in detail.

The CLASS project, a Government of India educational technology programme has followed a similar pattern as that of many of its predecessors. Three agencies, Department of Electronics, Department of Education and NCERT have been active partners for the project execution. On the receiving end were three types of schools, Kendriya Vidyalayas, State government run schools and Private/State aided schools. The two service giving agencies involved in the project were CMC and Resource Centres. This combination provided an intricate but a very difficult situation for the operation and management of the project.

Multiple Communications with Little Coordination

While it is recognized that multiple communications would ensure that messages would be received for action, in this case it created "information overload" for the principals of the schools who were probably not in the habit of receiving too many instructions on the same matter. Also, these messages were contradictory and resulted in confusing situations. In Madras, the instructions from the State Education Department were contradictory to what was communicated by the Department of Electronics or NCERT, New Delhi, on the issue of computer room air-conditioning. In case of Ahmedabad, a similar situation arose where a school had to remove the air-conditioner from the computer room upon the insistence of the CMC engineers.

It is uniformly reported that while Kendriya Vidyalaya Sangathan received direct communications from NCERT and also uniform instructions from Kendriya Vidyalaya Sangathan about the CLASS project, the other State run schools did not. The communications had to go through the State Government hierarchies or personnel with their strictly defined limits of jurisdiction. All communications were in writing and normal postal delays led to non-achievement of goals. Also, it seems there was no systematic pattern of communication between agencies themselves and CLASS project schools. As a result there was a lot of delay in installing the computers and disbursal of funds.

At the highest level, there seemed to have been lack of appropriate coordination between different agencies of the Government of India, reflecting on the overall functioning of the project. For example, all school principals complained about multiply queries on the same issue by several agencies involved in the implementation and evaluation of the CLASS project.

The management of the CLASS project has left a lot to be desired especially at the higher levels. In the absence of any clear-out instructions from implementing agencies to schools, the school authorities managed the CLASS project in their school as per their convenience. As a result, the pattern of management of the CLASS project was not uniform.

Lack of State Participation

In the planning and execution stage, the role of the respective State Education Departments, Assistant Commissioners, and Kendriya Vidyalaya Sangathan seems to be important. They were the main link between NCERT and CLASS project schools. At the execution stage, the district education authorities have to play equally important roles. Selection of schools, initiation of the process of selection of computer teachers, arrangement for their deputation for training at Resource Centres, provision of release of grants received from Government of India besides keeping the schools informed about latest developments were the functions of the respective State Department of Education. However, as far as it could be ascertained, except for written communications and instructions on different issues, State Government officials of the Education Department did not visit any of the schools to enquire about the way in which the CLASS project was implemented and managed. In most cases concerned district officials were not in the picture. Somewhat similar picture emerged in case of Kendriya Vidyalaya also.

Resource Centres

One of the important components of CLASS project was Resource Centre which carried out specific functions outlined by NCERT. Some of these functions included advice, support and consultancy to computer teachers; monitor and ensure proper implementation; ensure computer teacher growth and evolve an effective communication with schools. Besides, the Resource Centre was supposed to conduct initial and advanced training for computer teachers from time to time. Table 8.1 provides the location of Resource Centres in the six study clusters.

TABLE 8.1 : Location of Resource Centres in the Six Study Clusters

Sr. No.	Name of the City	Name of Resource Centre
1.	Ahmedabad	L.D. Engineering College
2.	Allahabad	Motilal Nehru Regional Engineering College
3.	Bhubaneshwar	Utkal University
4.	Delhi	(a) IIT (b) NCERT (c) Delhi University
5.	Guwahati	Assam Engineering College
6.	Madras	Department of Computer Science and Engineering, IIT

All Resource Centres have a Project Coordinator and a Project Fellow to look the affairs of CLASS project. The Coordinator is usually a senior faculty of the department where the Resource Centre is situated. The Project Fellows are usually fresh Engineering graduates with a specialization in computer hardware technology.

According to NCERT specifications, the Resource Centre personnel should undertake a week's training with a view to get acquainted with the major objectives and modalities of the CLASS project and develop a suitable training programme for computer teachers. All Resource Centres conducted at least two initial trainings with the exception of Allahabad where only one training was conducted. The advanced training programme for computer teachers already having initial training were conducted by Resource Centres at Delhi and Madras out of six centres. The Resource Centres at Madras, Delhi and Ahmedabad did conduct some workshops and training programmes of short duration for principals of computer schools, personnel from CMC, Kendriya Vidyalaya Sangathan and State Government, to provide a general idea about the CLASS project.

Resources Centres' Evaluation of Training and Trainees

The personnel of the Madras Resource Centre, appreciated the broad aims and objectives of CLASS project but were critical of the lack of planning and organisation in the implementation of the project. They felt that the CLASS project was initiated in a hurry without adequately providing any understanding of the project objectives and scope to agencies involved. According to these personnel, the next phase of CLASS project was being introduced in routine manner without assessing the pilot phase.

The Madras Resource Centre personnel felt that teachers had very high expectations of the training. The computer teachers expected to be taught advanced computer languages like COBOL, PASCAL, FORTRAN, whereas CLASS project envisaged the imparting of elementary skills to operate a computer with a given software package and to prepare simple programmes in BASIC. A mismatch certainly seems to have developed between the expectations of the computer teachers and the Resource Centres.

Except Madras, the Resource Centre personnel at other five places regarded the training as adequate. They also felt that the training imparted, including the course content and time duration, was sufficient. As mentioned earlier, the computer teachers did not seem to have sufficient knowledge of the aims of the CLASS project which led to very different expectations. Resource Centre personnel were generally critical about the computer teacher trainees' attitude towards training. They felt that with the exception of a few really interested and motivated individuals, none of the computer teacher trainees really took pains to learn and understand computer. In Delhi and Guwahati, it was found that the older teachers were motivated while in Allahabad, the younger teachers were generally found to be enthusiastic about the training. Lady teachers were generally found to be well motivated and interested during the computer training. In Ahmedabad the computer teachers from the State run schools were not interested in learning computer.

Interaction between Resource Centres and CLASS Project School

There was hardly any interaction between Resource Centre and schools except for the visit of Resource Centres personnel to schools at the time of the installation of computers and a few very far in between visits of the Project Fellow. Delhi Resource Centre differed in this matter. The Project Fellow in Delhi visited each school regularly, that is, thrice in two months. The major physical difficulty faced here was the large number of schools attached to the Resource Centre and long distances between schools.

The school authorities in six cities felt that the Resource Centre personnel should visit the schools on a regular basis atleast initially, when the schools might have some problem with hardware or software. On their part, the Resource Centre personnel stated that the schools were required to take initiative and visit the Resource Centre regularly to seek their assistance.

Some of the important functions of Resource Centres as outlined by NCERT and mentioned at the beginning of the chapter were not effectively carried out by the Resource Centres. The reason given for this state of affairs by the Project Coordinators was lack of time as they were full time faculty members of University/College departments and CLASS project was an additional responsibility. But, even the Project Fellow seemed to lack any initiative or interest in the CLASS project although they were specifically appointed to look after the affairs of the project.

The Resource Centres by and large had provided immediate assistance in case of replacement of faulty computer hardware on the same date, though, the latter steps of repair were not immediately carried out. There was delay at times in reporting the faulty component to CMC and also delay in informing the schools later on about the repaired piece. The Resource Centres contacted the CMC usually when some faulty computer component required repairs.

Resource Centre and Hardware

The computers provided for CLASS project at the Resource Centre were used by students of the concerned Departments. None of the programmes developed by these students were meant for CLASS project. The reason according to the Resource Centre personnel was lack of time and expertise in writing such programmes. The Resource Centre personnel at Madras and Ahmedabad made use of the software provided for CLASS project to draft letters and store information regarding the project.

Resource Centres and CLASS Project Agencies

The problem of multiple communication was faced by the Resource Centres also. The lack of coordination between Resource Centres and many agencies involved in the CLASS project, forced the Resource Centres to correspond on the same matter with different agencies or answer the same queries to different agencies.

As the Resource Centres were attached to educational institutions, they became part of the management hierarchy which at times created problems that could have been avoided had they been an independent body. The allotment of schools under the Resource Centres seemed to have taken place without any serious thought or consultation. Schools not only in the same city but also at far-away distances were placed under one Resource Centre. An example of the haphazard allotment is the placing of the CLASS projects school in Ankleshwar under Ahmedabad Resource Centre. Ankleshwar is nearer to Baroda which also has a Resource Centre, and utilizing its services could have been more convenient for this school. A similar example has been cited from Madras also. One cannot help wondering whether or not any rational method of allotment of CLASS project schools to Resource Centres was evolved.

Resource Centres and CMC

The Madras Resource Centre personnel were not happy with the services provided by the Madras CMC. So was the case in Bhubaneshwar. It was felt that the CMC engineers' lethargy led to delays in installation and repair work of computers. They also suggested that the schools should interact directly with CMC for rectifying hardware problems. This would save time as well as reduce the botheration for the Resource Centres. The Madras Resource Centre coordinator strongly felt that a full time CMC staff member should be appointed in a nodal office to take care of the CLASS project.

The School and CLASS Project

The quality of implementation of CLASS project cannot be assessed without taking into account the overall quality of management of other academic programmes in each school. It is but natural to expect that if a school is efficiently run and the academic schedule is well-organized and regular, the CLASS project should also be well-organized. On the other hand, if the general climate of academic work and discipline are not conducive, the CLASS project cannot in isolation, have a satisfactory run. The computer, which in a way represents the ultimate in contemporary technological innovation came to the school at a time when their resources and prescribed methods of teaching had little scope for incorporating even more humbler innovations.

In the immediate school context, the principal is the key figure in administration and the quality of his/her involvement has a lot to do with the success or failure of any educational project. Some principals gave weightage to the regular classes as compared to the computer classes. The principals also felt uncomfortable by various instructions received from various agencies attached to CLASS project. The general lack of initiative on the part of the principals can be attributed to the following reasons:

1. They felt more responsible about the actual course subjects of the prescribed syllabus. Unless this was covered, the principal may have to face allegation of incompetent management. Class project to team was an experimental exercise, the success or failure of which was not going to make them accountable.
2. Computer class was not part of the regular work load of the computer teacher. There being no incentive in any form, the principals were unable to press the computer teachers to devote time for the computer class.
3. A basic difficulty in getting greater commitment of the principals in the CLASS project appeared to be in the method

of establishing contact with them by the concerned agencies. All that was done to involve the principals were a series of official letters, instructions, guidelines and queries. The only communication between the CLASS project agencies and the principals was an impersonal 'file-contact'. The motivation and commitment of the principals could perhaps have been better obtained if they too were brought within the purview of discussion groups or workshops on how best to implement and administer the CLASS project in their respective schools. The whole procedure of management was such that the principal was merely an agent of correspondence and played post office function. The principal was responsible for the submission of final accounts as the grants were made available to him/her.

Interpersonal relationships between the principal-computer teachers and computer teachers-teachers also affected the management of CLASS project. A healthy working relationship between these individuals could have created an environment for better management of CLASS project.

Disbursal of CLASS Project Funds

There was invariably a long gap between the first letter from the Department of Education, Government of India, indicating disbursal of project funds and their actual distribution to the schools. The waiting period for the State Government run schools and Government aided/Private schools, was several months more than that of the Kendriya Vidyalayas. At the same time, the need for money was felt more by these very schools than the Kendriya Vidyalayas. Initial sanction of Rs. 4,000 per school by the Department of Electronics for this purpose was sliced down to Rs. 3,500 in order to provide Rs. 500 per school to NCERT to develop promotional material. This did create some confusion in the individual school principals and computer teachers who came to know about it. For example, it was also observed that a State run school in Guwahati, came to know the release of Rs. 3,500 as late as March 1986 through a letter dated March 19, 1986 from the Deputy Director of Secondary Education, Government of Assam. The same holds true in Allahabad, where the selection of a computer school or intermediate college could not be finalized due to lack of appropriate information (Agrawal, Sinha and Mullick 1986:30-31).

Another issue which must be discussed in this regard is the disbursal of funds to Resource Centres. In Madras, it was observed that the release of funds to the Resource Centre was handled simultaneously by both NCERT and the Department of Education, Government of India. On November 19, 1984, the NCERT wrote to Secretary of Education, Government of Tamil Nadu, dispatching Rs. 30,000 meant for the Resource Centre at the PSG College of Engineering, Coimbatore (Rs. 20,000 to meet the travelling allowances of the resource personnel and the reachers and Rs. 10,000 for preparing lessons and stationary). After a fortnight, on December 4, 1984, Rs. one lakh for meeting the cost of teacher training and detailed instructions on the CLASS project were sent to some of the Resource Centres by the Department of Education Government of India. When both the sums are meant for the same purpose, it is unclear why two different agencies should handle it. Similar observations were made in other cities.

The whole procedure followed for the disbursal of the funds was equally cumbersome leading to serious difficulties to an extent that during 1984-85, the same could not be utilized in the majority of the schools. There seems to be an information gap between Government of India and State Governments about the disbursal of the funds and more so as to how funds should be used by the school authorities. Even today, there is a need for clear instructions about the procedures to be followed for the utilization of the funds.

NCERT and CLASS Project

Several observations indicated that NCERT, New Delhi—the CLASS project implementing agency on behalf of Department of Education, Government of India, played an active monitoring role. This equally holds true for other places. But other agencies also duplicated the effort as is clear from the following observation from Madras.

Reddy and Sujatha (1986) reported that having entrusted the matter of disbursing supportive funds to the NCERT, the Department of Education, Government of India, continued to play parallel monitoring role. Both NCERT and the Department of Education, Government of India wrote expressing concern about the delay in the funds, reaching the schools. For instance, the Department of Education,

Government of India in the letter dated February 14, 1985 and the NCERT in the letter dated February 15, 1985, wrote on the same subject. Similarly, the NCERT was actively involved in the matter of installation of the computers in schools. Both agencies again wrote expressing their concern about the delay in installation of computers. (The NCERT in the month of March 1985 and the Department of Education, Government of India, in the month of July 1985). Though, their concern was understandable, such multiple communications created a lot of confusion and unnecessary tension for the schools.

Scheduling of Computer Classes

CLASS Project in the pilot phase was introduced in the school system as a non-examination subject. It was proposed that the computer classes be arranged against SUPW period and also be taken on Sundays and other holidays. Thirty hours of lectures and a minimum of 60 hours exposure per student per year in form of practical sessions was thought necessary.

Arrangement of computer classes within or outside the school time table proved to be a most difficult task for the schools. They tackled the problem by scheduling the computer classes as per their own convenience. Table 8.2 gives the arrangement of computer classes by the schools in all study clusters.

Majority of the schools had managed to accommodate the computer classes within the existing framework of time tables. SUPW periods were substituted by computer classes in Kendriya Vidyalayas whereas this arrangement was not available in case of other schools. So, they utilized games, library, Physical Training (PT) or assembly periods for the purpose. None of the Kendriya Vidyalayas held classes outside school hours, which was the case in some of the other schools except Delhi and Madras. Schools in Guwahati had not made any specific arrangement for computer classes in the time table as all available periods were allotted for teaching regular courses subjects. Free periods were ulilised for CLASS project purpose, so, there was no regularity of holding classes. A number of reasons were cited for the reluctance of the computer teachers to hold classes after school hours. By conducting computer classes after school hours, the teacher felt that they were unable to attend to their personal work or tuitions. Tuitions have become a lucrative business for school teachers especially in Ahmedabad where

TABLE 8.2 : Scheduling of Computer Classes in School Time Table

Sr. No.	Name of the City	Computer Class Timing			
		Within School Hours	Outside School Hours	Within and Outside School Hours	Total
1.	Ahmedabad	83.3	16.7	–	100.0
2.	Allahabad	50.0	25.0	25.0	100.0
3.	Bhubaneshwar	75.0	25.0	–	100.0
4.	Delhi	100.0	–	–	100.0
5.	Guwahati	20.0	80.0	–	100.0
6.	Madras	100.00	–	–	100.0
	Percentage	83.0	14.6	2.1	100.0
	Total	40	7	1	48

most of the senior school teachers use all their spare time before and after school hours in taking tuitions. The heads of the school and computer teachers also felt that the parents of the children might object to the extra classes after school, particularly if the students were girls who had to reach home early. Another reason which might possibly apply here was no monetary incentive was available to the computer teachers expect for the travelling allowance from the contingency amount of Rs. 3,500. One of the schools in Ahmedabad tackled this problem by paying the teachers an honorarium from the school trust for working outside school hours.

Software Packages—Relevance to School Curriculum

Only a few software packages have been found to be relevant to the school curriculum. In fact, CLASS project or Computer Based Learning packages are more relevant to lower classes. The Kendriya Vidyalaya students generally found the syllabus quite below their standards. On general view that prevails is that the CLASS project should be expanded to supplement the teaching of regular subjects instead of merely learning to operate the computer for general use. Irrespective of their level of motivation towards CLASS project, the computer teachers feel that more and more software packages suited to the regular school curriculum must be supplied. The report from

Madras states that " even in schools where CLASS was discarded in favour of Computer Science—elective/optional subject, a few packages have been shown to the students as a prelude to teaching them things that can be done with a computer and in an attempt to familiarize the students with the elementary operations on a computer" (Subha Reddy and Sujatha 1986 : 83). It was also felt that the software packages would do more justice if they were in the local language as students reading in schools other than English medium cannot easily comprehend the language of the software. In the day-to-day working even in Kendriya Vidyalayas, either Hindi is used by the students or the language of the State. As indicated earlier even some computer teachers during their training had this difficulty. This problem of communication could be solved by preparing indigenous software suited to the local needs, also keeping in mind the study curriculum of the class for which it is being prepared. Such an effort is essential if computer is to be demystified for the students of all sections of the society.

9

COST-BENEFIT ASPECTS OF CLASS PROJECT

By U.K. Srivastava

Both qualitative and quantitative results about computer demystification were presented in the last two chapters. In this chapter the cost aspect of the CLASS project has been analyzed.

Initially 500 computers including peripherals (monitors, printers, floppy-discs and cassette recorders) were a gift from the United Kingdom, as these did not require any payment. The cost of subsequent systems in the expansion phase will have to be met by the Government of India. In addition, the CLASS project schools received from NCERT Rs. 3,500 as lumpsum installation cost. As indicated in chapter VIII, NCERT kept Rs. 500 per school for the promotional work. The same is not included here. Similarly, the cost of CMC maintenance has been included in the cost analysis. The repair and maintenance of the computer and any replacement of peripherals was made by CMC and the Resource Centres. The computer schools were supposed to bear the operating cost of the computers

In the a *priori* analysis of the total investment (irrespective of who pays for it), operating cost and the number of students expected to be exposed to the computers, following assumptions were made.

(i) The initial investment in computers including the installation cost of Rs. 3,500 comes to Rs. 83,500;

(ii) The floppy discs costing Rs. 1,788 need to be replaced every three years. The monitors, printers and cassette recorders have a life of five years. The replacement cost comes to Rs. 6,333;

(iii) The operating cost of computers (for about 630 hours per computer plus about Rs. 250 for other miscellaneous cost) comes to Rs. 1000 per annum for two computers in a school;

(iv) It is expected that about 30 students will work on each computer in two batches of three at a time. Therefore, it is expected that about 60 students will be exposed to computer at each school;

(v) The life of the CPU is expected to be about 10 years. At the end of 10 years, one can expect 10 per cent of the initial investment as salvage value (recovery from disposal of used computers is estimated to be Rs. 5,000 for each computer); and

(vi) If the above mentioned investment and operating cost are discounted at 10 per cent, the present value of the total comes to Rs. 88,272 for the total life of 10 years. This means on *a priori* basis the cost of exposure per student comes to Rs. 148. The detailed calculations are indicated in Table 9.1

In addition, some of the schools at least were expected to incure out of packet costs in terms of honorarium to computer teachers. Also, there are costs of administration and monitoring of CLASS project and the expenses incurred on the Resource Centres. All these were to be taken into account in arriving at the actual cost of computer exposure after the collection of the actual data from the schools. It

TABLE 9.1 : Investment in Two Computer Systems, Replacement of Peripherals, Operational Costs and Present Value of Total Costs

Year	Investment (Rs.)	Operating Costs (Rs.)	Total Cost (Rs.)	Discount Factor	Present Value (Rs.)
0	83,500	—	80,000	.000000	80,000
1	—	1,000*	1,000	.909091	909
2	—	1,000	1,000	.826446	826
3	—	1,000	1,000	.751316	751
4	1,788	1,000	2,788	.683013	1,904
5	—	1,000	1,000	.620921	621
6	6,338	1,000	7,338	.564474	4,142
7	—	1,000	1,000	.513158	513
8	1,788	1,000	2,788	.466507	1,301
9	—	1,000	1,000	.424098	424
10	—	1,000	1,000	.385543	386
11	–8,000	—	–8,000	.350494	–2,804
Present Value					Rs. 88,973

$$\text{Cost per Student} = \frac{\text{Present Value}}{\text{600 Students}} = \frac{88973}{600} = \text{Rs. } 148.24$$

* Includes Rs. 200 per computer year on electricity consumption for 630 hours (at the rate 300 Watts per hour) and Re. 1 for KW, Rs. 200 as cost of dusting, cleaning, etc., per year and Rs. 400 by way of repairs and maintenance per year.

was also expected that the analysis of actual data would indicate the variations in costs and number of students actually exposed to computer among three school types.

Besides the cost data, an assessment of benefits was also to be done in the form of : (i) demystification of computer students who were exposed to the computers; and (ii) overall multiplier effects in terms of awareness and motivation on the part of the members of the community connected to those exposed to computers.

Data from CLASS Project Schools

Data related to cost could be obtained from 105 CLASS project schools. These included 36 Kendriya Vidyalayas, 36 State Government run schools and 33 State aided/private schools. The operating cost items include electricity, honorarium to computer teachers and even salary/wages to peons. In case of State aided/private schools and even State Government run schools, honorarium to computer teachers and wages to peons was the most important items of operating cost (see Table 9.2). Annual operating cost of the computer was estimated to be Rs. 1,865 in Kendriya Vidyalayas, Rs. 11,677 in State Government run schools and Rs. 16,107 in State aided/private schools. Overall sample average came to Rs. 9,883.

The survey covered first year of operation, which was in a way a period of adjustment. On an average the computer was down for 16 days a year (see Table 9.3). The situation was no better even in Kendriya Vidyalayas. The breakdown occurred due to various reasons (see Table 9.4).

On the basis of data from 172 CLASS project schools, it was observed that 57 students on an average were exposed to computers in each school. It was also observed that in case of State aided/private schools the number of students exposed to computers was much higher (73 per school) than Kendriya Vidyalayas (54 per school) and State Government run schools (44 per school) (see Table 9.3). *A priori* expectation was that in each school 60 students would be exposed to computers.

As against that *a priori* expectation, the actual exposure per student to hands-on-practice on computers was much lower. On an average the students got only 34 minutes for the hands-on-practice in the entire academic year. The impact of limited hands-on-practice in terms of time given to students is visible when it comes to the

TABLE 9.2 : Date on Operating Cost Per Year of CLASS Project

Sr. No.	School Management	Itemwise Average Cost Per Year Per School						Total Operating Cost on an Average per School per Year
		Electricity		Honorarium to Teachers		Wages to Peon		
		No. of Schools which Responded	Average Cost (Rs.)	No. of Schools which Responded	Average Cost (Rs.)	No. of Schools which Responded	Average Cost (Rs.)	
1.	Kendriya Vidyalaya	36	1,365	5	200	1	300	1,865
2.	State Government	36	1,872	13	7,735	6	2,070	11,677
3.	State Aided/Private	33	1,737	11	13,000	9	1,370	16,107
	Sample Average	105	1,658	29	6,978	16	1,247	9,883

TABLE 9.3. : Computer Operation and Actual Exposure per Student

Sr. No.	School Management	Down Time in Days	Total Operation Time in Minutes	Total No. of Students Exposed During the Year	Average No. of Students Exposed to Computer per School	Actual Exposure per Student in Minutes
1.	Kendriya Vidyalaya	1,122	99,240	3,328	54	30
2.	State Government	1,014	161,040	2,723	44	59
3.	State Aided/Private	592	58,560	3,290	73	18
	Total	2,728	318,840	9,341	57	34

assessment of benefits.

Given the objectives of computer literacy, the benefits were measured in two parts: (i) percentage of students who were exposed to computers and got demystified or partially demystified; and (ii) benefits to other members of the community. As explained in Chapter 7, demystification was measured on a 15 point scale.

As described in Chapter 7, a score of 11 was considered as the cut off point whereby those who scored 11 points and above on the scale were deemed to be demystified. Anyone who scored between 6 and 10 points was considered partially demystified. Those who scored 5 points and below were considered not demystified.

As indicated in Chapter VII, Table 7.9, data related to students' demystification were available from 268 students of Kendriya Vidyalayas, 192 students from State Government run schools and 84 students from State aided/private schools (see Table 9.5). The percentage of those computer students who were demystified to total exposed in the survey came as 19 per cent for Kendriya Vidyalayas; 17 per cent for the State Government run schools; and only 1.2 per cent in State aided/private schools. The percentage of the partially demystified students is 35 per cent for Kendriya Vidyalayas; 33 per cent for State Government run schools,, and 27 per cent for the State aided/private schools (see Table 9.5). Low percentage of those exposed and demystified indicated a limited computer exposure (in terms of hands-on-practice), software used, and perhaps lack of adequate training of computer teachers. As indicated in Chapter 8, CLASS project classes were not included as a part of curriculum. They were only part of SUPW and extra-curricular activities of the computer students.

As indicated in Chapter 8, Table 7.8, in addition to the computer students actually exposed to computers, information about the computer was found to have been disseminated to their parents, sisters and brothers, friends and neighbours (see Table 7.8). Although this benefit cannot be quantified, it has guaranteed the environment for motivating more students to take up computer as a career at a subsequently stage of their studies.

Estimated Cost of Computer Awareness

The estimated cost of computer operations consists of two parts : (i) fixed cost (imputed market price of computers); and (ii) operating cost (electricity + honorarium to teachers + wages to peons). Total intial fixed cost of Rs. 83,500 was annualized at the rate of 10 per

TABLE 9.4 : Information on the Repairs or Replacement of Parts

Sr. No.	School Management	Frequencies of Parts Repaired						
		VDU	CPU	Floppy Drive	Printer	Cassette Recorder	Voltage Stabilizer	Others
1.	Kendriya Vidyalaya	6	14	2	8	4	2	9
2.	State Government	4	18	2	9	3	3	10
3.	State Aided/Private	4	16	1	6	3	4	6
	Total	14	48	5	23	10	9	25

Note : The Cost of repair of part and replacement is not included.

TABLE 9.5 : Direct Benefits in Terms of Students Exposed to Computer and Demystification

Sr. No.	School Management	Number of Students Exposed	Total Exposure Time	Average Score of Demystification	Total Number of Students Considered Demystified	Total Number of Students Considered Partially Demystified	Percentage of Those Demystified to Total Exposed	Percentage of Those Partially Denystified to Total Exposed
1.	Kendriya Vidyalaya	268	37 hours 5 minutes	6.53	52	94	19.6	35.3
2.	State Government	192	52 hours 35 minutes	3.85	32	63	16.7	32.8
3.	State Aided/Private	84	33 hours 35 minutes	6.06	1	23	1.2	27.4
	Total	544	122 hours 55 minutes	5.51	85	180	15.6	33.1

TABLE 9.6 : Actual Cost of Computer Exposure per Student and per Demystified Student

Sr. No.	School Management	Number of Schools	Annualized Fixed Cost (a)	Operating Cost (includes 10% for maintenance & repair) (b)	Total Annual Cost (a + b)	Number of Students Exposed	Cost per Student Exposed	Number of Students Demystified	Cost per Demystified Student
1.	Kendriya Vidyalaya	62	13,610	1,865	15,475	54	287	10	1,547
2.	State Government	64	13,610	11,677	25,287	44	575	7	3,612
3.	State Aided/Private	46	13,610	16,107	29,718	73	407	1	29,718
	Sample Average	57	13,610	9,883	23,493	57	423	16	11,626

cent of capital cost and ten years of life of the computers (assumed). This cost comes to Rs. 13,610 in case of all types of schools (see Table 9.6). The operating cost varies among the types of schools by management. Accordingly, total annual cost varies also between the type of school (see Table 9.6). When this cost is seen in terms of the students actually exposed, the calculations indicate that the cost per student (actually exposed to computer) ranges between Rs. 287 in Kendriya Vidyalayas to Rs. 575 in State Government run schools. These cost estimates are substantially higher than those made on *a priori* basis (see Table 9.1).

If we further view these costs in the light of actual number of students actually demystified (as per the objectives of CLASS project), the costs per student are astronomical. The estimated cost per demystified student ranges between Rs. 1,547 in Kendriya Vidyalayas, Rs. 3,612 in Government run schools and Rs. 29,718 in State aided private/public schools. This conclusion emerges because of very low percentage of students exposed to computer.

Large number of days of down time of computers stresses the need to examine the back up service provided by the CMC and Resource Centres. Computers have created very strong multiplier effects which is good for motivating more and more students to develop interest in computers to broaden the educational base. The concern with the cost effectiveness of CLASS project and the above conclusion and findings indicated the following areas of policy actions to be taken:

(a) There is a need for a strong monitoring system to provide information on mid course correction. The key variables to be monitored are as follows: (i) number of students actually exposed to computer (including the assimilation of computer classes in the main curriculum); (ii) the actual time of exposure and problems with software and instructions imparted; (iii) efficiency of computer teachers' training for the purpose; and (iv) working of the CMC and Resource Centres in repair and maintaining the computers and provision of software;

(b) There is a need to strengthen the computer teachers' training to make CLASS project more effective. There is also a need to provide incentives to computer teachers who are assigned the task; and

(c) There is a need to evolve an organizational mechanism to intiate corrective action within the CLASS project schools found to be deficient with respect to the key variables for the sources of the project.

10

CLASS PROJECT IN RETROSPECTIVE

In this book the aim was to analyze the extent to which the computer demystification took place among the students of higher secondary schools as a result of CLASS project. Both qualitative and quantitative methods were used to evaluate the level of computer demystification and factors influencing the process of computer demystification. An attempt was also made to have the cost-benefit analysis of the CLASS project. Based on the total analysis, major conclusions and recommendations are provided in this chapter. It is hoped that these recommendations will help in the future planning of CLASS project in its expansion phase. Also, it will help in the planning and implementation of similar other educational technology projects. Some efforts have been also made to carry the current debate on computer literacy and methods of evaluation of such educational technology project.

In the introductory chapter, the most important objective outlined for the evaluation relates to "computer demystification". The computer demystification was operationally defined in terms of knowledge about computer operation and use (see Chapter 3). Analysis shows that computer demystification is closely associated with the amount of exposure the students had. Factors inhibiting computer exposure throw light as to how the CLASS project was implemented and managed.

Due to lack of lead time and appropriate coordination for the implementation of the CLASS project, in spite of best intentions of the project implementors, computers could not be installed in schools, thus causing delay in the starting of the CLASS project. The delay period varied from one month to a whole year. Therefore, it is recommended that the lead time before starting the project must be kept in view while planning a project in the field of educational technology. It is suggested that about 150 days of lead time would be minimum to initiate a new project.

Given the geographical diversity and intricacies of educational bureaucracy, the existence of an intermediary agency as a focal point is most desirable for appropriate implementation of the project. In CLASS project, Resource Centres were created for this purpose but they played a marginal role. Revitalization of Resource Centres to play an effective role both in the installation phase and at a later stage to ensure the smooth running of CLASS project is essential. The Resource Centre should be persuaded to play an active role and should be in a position to interact with the computer schools at working level.

Recognition of "micro" planning in a project like CLASS should form an essential component of the total project plan. This will ensure end to end completion of the project. Otherwise, there would be an appreciable gap as seen between what is technically known as 'installation' according to CMC engineers and 'operational' according to the computer teachers. Same may be said about the disbursal of project funds given to each school. In the absence of detailed guidelines for expenditure of funds, many computer schools could not spend the money and in the process the project suffered. It is, therefore, recommended that micro planning must be done for similar projects.

One of the major impediments in the smooth implementation of CLASS project was lack of coordination. No established method of appropriate linkages among various agencies working on the project, duplication of effort and lack of single chain of command was observed in CLASS project. It is, therefore, suggested that in expansion phase of CLASS project or for any such educational technology projects, there is a need for serious consideration to create a project office with full responsibility and authority for coordination and efficient implementation of such projects.

The CLASS project schools, regardless of management type, faced a great deal of difficulty in incorporating computer classes in the regular time table of the school. Analyses have shown that school authorities had to cut corners to incorporate computer classes in the regular school time table. Typically computer classes were arranged as a substitute for Socially Useful and Productive Work (SUPW) and classes meant for sports and other extra-curricular activities. By and large, no computer classes were arranged beyond normal school hours, thereby limiting the computer use. Given the present syllabus load, it is not possible to incorporate computer literacy into the existing educational system even if it promises a bright career opportunity to the students. Hence, it is suggested that computer education should be incorporated in the syllabus as done in Tamil Nadu after appropriate adjustment and reduction in the existing syllabus.

The lukewarm attitude of the principals, perceived imposition of additional work on computer teachers were deterrents in effective implementation of CLASS project. Further, no direct involvement of the school management or educational bureaucracy and above all no gain or profit as incentive to anyone, created a condition in which the CLASS project in its first academic year 1984-85 of running remained a non-starter. Even in the second year, CLASS project moved slowly. Subsequent visits to computer schools indicated reduction in the enthusiasm for holding computer classes. What does it all amount to? A project that attracted national attention of educational planners, policy-makers and technologists could not come upto the expectations. It calls for necessary pre-project study, contextual understanding of educational needs and system and proper marriage of the two.

The key actor for the effective implementation of CLASS project was the computer teacher. All the computer teachers were drawn from the existing teaching staff of the schools. Based on some pre-conceived notion that science background was required for computer teaching and learning the science teachers were selected. Seniority being another criterion for the selection in most places, there was preponderance of computer teachers in their mid career having 31 to 50 years of age. Even though, the computer teachers felt happy and proud to be associated with the CLASS project, their school work load, and other problems of the project adversely affected their performance.

The computer teachers by and large felt that they were not adequately trained to handle the computer. On the top of it, there was a time gap of more than a year between the initial training and the actual commencement of the project in majority of the schools. The net effect was that the computer teachers were constrained in imparting adequate computer training to the students. It is suggested that rational criteria based on interest and aptitude should be evolved for the selection of the computer teachers. The selected teachers should be given adequate and timely training to be effective in such an educational project. Methods should be evolved to provide "incentives" to such teachers for sustaining their interest in the project. In the long run, it will be essential to have separate trained computer teachers for teaching computer. Some efforts should be made in this direction.

Inappropriate selection of teachers, inadequate training, large time gap between training and actual computer use, confusion about the aims of CLASS project and its place in the school curriculum had its toll on the quality of computer teaching. To some extent, it created hostility against computer among those teachers who thought that imparting basic knowledge in the prescribed subjects was essential rather than allowing students to "play" with the computers. Such teachers were of the view that the investment in computers was a waste of resource which could be better utilized in providing basic amenities, equipment and books to schools lacking in these, thereby raising the educational standard and benefiting the poor students.

In the planning and execution stage, active role of the respective State Education Departments and Assistant Commissioners in case of Kendriya Vidyalaya Sangathan and district education authorities seems to be important. But in CLASS project they were mostly not in the picture. Direct involvement of these officials at all stages of implementation is suggested to minimize delays and help effective execution.

There was a lack of flow of information at various levels regarding different aspects of CLASS project. There is a need for a fast and smooth flow of information to facilitate effective functioning of CLASS project or for that matter any such project involving a large number of professionals and administrators.

Two aspects of the computer teaching—learning that attracted the attention are computer software and method and medium of teaching computer. As only few computer classes were held it was difficult to discern any pattern of computer teaching in this study. In absence of any prescribed course outline, computer teachers took individual decisions about the pedagogy of teaching computer. While this provided flexibility, it also created difficulties both for the computer teachers and students. Except 'WELCOME' software package many of the other software packages were not tried out by majority of the computer students. The other problem was English as the language of software packages. The students of State Government and Private/Public government aided schools had difficulty in understanding English.

The computer teachers recommended a clear teaching

syllabus for the success of CLASS project. They also drew attention to the need for more rigour in selection of computer teachers to eliminate those on the verge of retirement. Availability of indigenous software according to some teachers would be advantageous to non-English medium students.

On the whole, the level of demystification was found to be low. The main reason being that few computer classes than prescribed were held. In some cases, a large number of students attended a single computer class, thereby reducing the positive impact of learning. Understanding of English language, the medium of computer teaching in some schools was a problem and most important of all, many of the teachers themselves were not demystified.

The analysis indicated that students were keen to learn computers but they got very little exposure. Not more than 15 per cent students got demystified in the academic year 1985-86. The problem did not lie with the students who showed positive inclination towards learning computers, but lay with the planning, implementation and management of the CLASS project. It also requires rigorous changes in the management of the programme that will provide better scheduling in the school time table for computer teaching incentives to teachers and involvement of various educational functionaries, both at the state and district levels.

Due to limited exposure of computer to the students in which neither software nor hardware were utilized to any extent, it is difficult to carry any discussion whether computer can be an aid to the existing educational system? Is there a particular discipline of knowledge in which computer can be used meaningfully? Can computer help equalize the learning opportunities? While some answers were found in the Euro-American context, it is difficult to give ~~any~~ such recommendation from the CLASS evaluation study. Further experimentation would be required for this purpose. The methodologies followed for the present evaluation amply supported the view that both holistic and survey methods can be meaningfully utilized in the Indian context. These have provided broader as well as insightful understanding of educational technology project.

Since the introduction of CLASS project, in less than five years, computer learning has caught the imagination of national entrepreneurs and multinational computer companies. Among the three technologies, photocopying system, video and now computer have invaded courtrooms and classrooms alike. The piece of computer hardware whether in use, has become an office "show-piece". The same holds true for schools and colleges of India. There is no doubt that it has helped to create a new environment in education, helped acquire a new skill to make an individual an efficient person in the international world of science and education. The question asked as to who is taking the advantage of the computer? and who are the people who are pushing and selling the "computer knowledge"? The answer is a selected social class; economically and educationally in position to buy the "computer knowledge". Therefore, the computer thrust is going in the direction of helping those who are socially and educationally in an advantageous position. If left to the market forces, as it is seen in the last couple of years, the computer knowledge gap will further increase. However, government intervention having committed to provide equal educational opportunity may help stabilize the situation if not reverse the situation. Though, this study does not attempt to answer the long-term societal implications of educational technology introduction, it does hint that the benefit of computer literacy seems to be in favour of the "well-off" in the society. Hence, keeping the educational policy of the country in view, efforts are required to provide equal opportunity for computer learning.

BIBLIOGRAPHY

Adams, Tony, 1988, Computers in Learning: A Coat of Many Colours. In *Computers and Education*, Vol. 12, No.1, PPL Computer Assisted Learning: Selected Proceedings from the CAL'87 Symposium ed. M.R. Kibby and J.T. Mayes.

Agrawal, Binod C. (ed), 1985, *Anthropological Methods for Communication Research*, New Delhi, Concept Publishing Company.

Agrawal, Binod and Arbind K. Sinha assisted by R. Mullick, 1986, CLASS Project Report on 'Computer Demystification in School : An Evaluative Study'. Ahmedabad : Development and Educational Communication Unit.

Agrawal, Binod C., Anita Kamdar and Sulbha Khanna, 1986, CLASS Project Report on 'Computer Impact on Students: An Evaluation'. Ahmedabad : Development and Educational Communication Unit.

Anonymous, 1984, Report of the National Workshop on Computer Literacy Curriculum Held at NCERT on 26-27 March, 1984. New Delhi: NCERT.

Bhagabati, Annada C. and Meenakshi Das, 1986, Evaluation of Computer Literacy and Studies in Schools (CLASS) in Guwahati. Unpublished Project Report Sponsored by DECU, ISRO, Ahmedabad.

Bhandari, J.S., 1986, Computer Literacy and Studies in Schools (CLASS) in Delhi : An Evaluation of CLASS Project through Holistic Study. Unpublished Project Report Sponsored by DECU, ISRO, Ahmedabad.

Burns, P.K. and W.C. Bozeman, 1981, Computer-Assisted-Instruction and Mathematics Achivement: Is There a Relationship? In *Educational Technology*, 1981: 32-39.

Chambers, J.A and J.W. Sprecher, 1980, Computer Assisted Instruction: Current Trends and Critical Issues. *Communications of the ACM* 23(6): 232-243.

Chandra, Ashok, 1984, Preface to the Report on the National Workshop on Computer Literacy Curriculum. New Delhi: NCERT.

Development and Educational Communication Unit (DECU), 1985, Computer Literacy and Studies in Schools (CLASS) Evaluation: An Interim Report. Ahmedabad: DECU.

Edward, J. *et.al.*, 1975, How Effective is CAI? A Review of the Research. In *Educational Leadership*, 1975: 147-153.

Fisher, Glenn, 1984, Where CAI is Effective. A Summary of the Research. In *Electronic Learning*, Vol. 3(3): 82-84.

Foreman, Denyse, 1980, Search of the Literature. *In* Instructional Use of Microcomputer : A Report on BBC Pilot Project.

Hartley, S.S., 1977, Meta-analysis of the Effects of Individually Paced Instruction in Mathematics. Doctoral Dissertation, University of Colorado.

Jernstedt, C.G., 1985, Computer Enhanced Collaborative Learning: A New Technology for Education. *In Micro Computers for Basic and Vocational Skills*, University of Massachussetts.

Kearsley, G.P., 1976, Some Facts about CAI. *Journal of Educational Data Processing*, 13(3): 1-11.

Kling, R., 1984, Assimilating Social Values in Computer Based Technologies in Telecommunication Policy. *Tele-communication Policy*, 1984; 127-147.

Kulik, J.A., 1981, Integrating Findings from Different Levels on Instruction. Paper presented at the American Educational Research Association Meeting, Los Angeles, April 1981.

Kulik, J.A., B. Robert L,G.W. Williams, 1983, Effects of Computer Based Teaching on Secondary School Students. *Journal of Educational Psychology*, Vol. 75(1): 19-26.

Kulik, J.A. *et. al.,* 1980, Effectiveness of Computer Based College Teaching: A Meta-analysis of Findings. *Review of Eucational Research*, Vol. 50(4): 525-544.

Lal, R.B. and Madhavi Joshi, 1986, Computer Education in School: Evaluation of Computer Litercay and Studies in School Pilot Project. A Holistic Study. Unpublished Project Report Sponsored by DECU, ISRO, Ahmedabad.

Luehrmann, A., 1980, Computer Literacy Analysis and a Solution for it. *In B.Y.T.E.*

Mahapatra, L.K. and Bandita Swain, 1986, Evaluation Report on the CLASS Project in Orissa. Unpublished Project Report Sponsored by DECU, ISRO, Ahmedabad.

Maheswari, S.N., 1984, Student and Teacher Training Curriculum. In Report of the National Workshop on Computer Literacy Curriculum. New Delhi: NCERT.

Malhotra, P.L., 1984, Director's Address *In* Report of the National Workshop on Computer Literacy Curriculum. New Delhi: NCERT.

Misra, Shashank, 1986, Final Report on the Holistic Study of the CLASS Project at Allahabad. Unpublished Project report Sponsored by DECU, ISRO, Ahmedabad.

Ragosta, M., P.W. Holland, D.T. Jamison, 1982, Computer Assisted Instruction and Compensatory Education: The ETS/LAUDS Study. Project Report of Educational Testing Service, Princeton, New Jersey.

Subba Reddy N. and G. Sujatha, 1986, Computer Literacy and Studies in Schools in Madras City: An Evaluation of the Pilot Phase of CLASS Project. Unpublished Project Report Sponsored by DECU, ISRO, Ahmedabad.

INDEX